The Crime Writer's Guide to Police Practice and Procedure

Michael O'Byrne started his police career in the 1960s, aged nineteen, in the Royal Hong Kong Police, serving there through Mao's cultural revolution. He then moved to London's Metropolitan Police, working in Notting Hill, the West End and New Scotland Yard before moving to Surrey then Thames Valley, ending his police career as Chief Constable in Bedfordshire.

The Crime Writer's Guide to Police Practice and Procedure

Michael O'Byrne

ROBERT HALE · LONDON

ISBN 978-0-7090-8631-4

Robert Hale Limited
Clerkenwell House
Clerkenwell Green
London EC1R 0HT

www.halebooks.com

A catalogue record for this book is available from the British Library

2 4 6 8 10 9 7 5 3 1

To Carole, proof reader, editor and general taskmaster.

Typeset in 11/14pt Palatino
by Derek Doyle & Associates, Shaw Heath
Printed and bound by the
MPG Books Group in the UK

CONTENTS

LIST OF FIGURES

INTRODUCTION

In 2007 I was asked to run a workshop on 'crime for writers' at the Swanwick Writers' School. It was clear from the number of people who attended that there was a large demand for a book on crime and police practice, aimed at the layperson, written in non-technical language and with a writer's perspective. I had been a police officer since the age of nineteen and had served in the Royal Hong Kong Police, London's Metropolitan Police, the Surrey Constabulary and the Thames Valley Police, and had ended up as Chief Constable of the Bedfordshire Police. I retired early in order to write and travel.

Following the workshop I looked around to see what there was to satisfy this need, only to find a dearth of material. The books available appear to be mainly memoirs by various ranks in which they described what they did but not how the mechanics of the criminal justice system works; and because they were focused on past lives the practices they did describe were out of date. I've been writing steadily since I retired, completing one book on the future of the police, *Changing Policing – Revolution Not Evolution*, and two crime thrillers, for which I have yet to find a publisher. My own writing has enabled me to see the system from the perspective of the writer who needs to maintain pace, develop characters, create conflict and sustain tension. This book will take you through the crime process in a logical sequence, pointing out the key issues, describing them in non-technical language from a writer's point of view.

The question that bugs every crime writer is how important is it for their book to reflect police practice. Every writer's objective is to draw the reader into your world, get them to suspend belief in the everyday and believe that the scenes you have created are real. If the bubble bursts, for whatever reason, the reader is lost and drifts back into reality, well-drawn characters become one-dimensional, a carefully constructed drama becomes melodrama and plot becomes mere artifice.

The purpose of this book is not to advise you to have your characters do exactly what police officers and the other people in the criminal justice process would do in real life; that would be tedious to write and boring to read. When thinking of how to describe its purpose I was reminded of an exchange between a barrister and a judge. The judge had shown that he was not particularly sympathetic to the barrister's point of view and was trying to move matters on. When the barrister asked to address him on a technical issue the judge made it clear that he did not see much point in it and held his head in his hands throughout the barrister's address.

At the end of the address he looked up and said, 'Well Mr Jones, at the end of that I'm no wiser.'

The barrister replied, 'Perhaps no wiser, sir, but certainly better informed.'

The purpose of the book is to help you be better informed – to describe what happens so that you can decide for yourself what you will use and where you will use your writer's licence, knowing how far you have departed from fact, and how far you can go and still maintain the magic bubble. It will enable you to do two things: first, to make an informed judgement on what your characters will do in your story; and secondly to show you the areas of tension and conflict that exist – the grit that lies at the heart of every novel's pearl – and maybe introduce you to one or two that have not yet been exploited.

CHAPTER 1

The Investigation Begins

In real life most unlawful killings require little in the way of detective skills. The victim and the killer are usually known to one another. The killing is an assault that goes wrong, that goes too far. The job of the detective is to gather the evidence needed for a conviction and ensure that all the legal hurdles are safely negotiated and that the case-building and subsequent trial take as little police time (the only truly scarce resource) as possible. Given the trauma of the victim's families and the killer it is surprising that so little is written using this scenario. Perhaps it is the difficulty of setting it into a genre – is it a crime novel or a novel in which a crime occurs?

The scenario used by most crime writers is very different. There it is usually a case of either who did it or how the detective can prove the case against the person they know did it. The purpose of this chapter is to describe police procedures in 'stranger' killings and at the end suggest some ways in which these procedures can be managed without slowing down the pace of the story or killing any tension between the characters.

Finding the Body

Winston Churchill said that the two most difficult things to do in life are to climb a wall that is leaning towards you and kiss a girl who is leaning away from you. For killers the two most difficult things are to carry out the killing unobserved or unrecognized and to get rid of the body. Put crudely the body is over a hundredweight of meat, in a package five to six feet long, which, in the key twenty-four hours after the killing will go rock solid through *rigor mortis* and then will begin to rot and to smell. In addition it is extremely difficult to move the body after the killing without this being identified in the post-mortem because of *livor mortis* or post-mortem lividity (the fact that blood will pool in the lowest part of the body after the heart stops pumping). The serial killer Dennis Nilsen was caught simply because his drains could not cope with the volume of material he was trying to dispose of. When confronted by police he still had the remains of several bodies in his flat.

Where the body is found is important to both the writer and the detective, as it is the first clue about the killer. First, the degree of premeditation. At one end of the scale is the 'domestic' killing where the body is almost always found where the death occurred. The killing is not premeditated and no thought has been given by the killer to the disposal of the body or how blame can be either mitigated or avoided completely. There are exceptional cases where the killer is quick enough on his or her feet to manage the task. An example is the 'Lady in the Lake' murder, when Gordon Park managed to dump his wife's body in Coniston Water in 1976 and persuade everyone that she had run off after an argument. He was incredibly unlucky that her body was found over twenty years later in 1997 (he still protests his innocence). At the other end of the scale the killer forces or lures the victim to a remote spot where the killing takes place and it is relatively easy to bury or otherwise hide the body.

If the victim is adult and the body has been moved then either the killer will be a man, as most women simply do not have the upper body strength required, or two or more people will have helped to move it. And, as we will see in Chapter 3, whatever was used to move the body will likely carry some trace.

The body is almost always found by a member of the public – a neighbour who was worried about the victim, a person out walking the dog. The first police officer on the scene is usually a uniformed patrol constable. The growing use of community support officers may mean that one (or more likely two or three) of them may now be the first. In writing terms this is a useful device for the mismanagement of the scene in the initial stages as CSOs do not have the same training or mind-set as police officers. The next officer to attend is the senior uniformed officer on duty, called appropriately enough the Duty Officer. In cities this is usually an inspector but in rural locations it is more likely to be a sergeant. This officer will supervise the securing of the scene, arranging the attendance of CID and beginning whatever local inquiries are possible with the officers immediately available.

In investigation terms the best body is one that is well and truly dead, as this means that fewer people will have had access to the crime scene before it is examined forensically. The worst scenario is where the victim is wounded and dying as this will mean that everyone and his uncle will be through the scene before the examination and the victim will have been removed to hospital. It has happened that the person finding the victim only calls the ambulance and not the police; by the time police arrive, having been alerted by the ambulance crew, not only has the victim gone to hospital but the helpful neighbours are busy cleaning up the blood! As we shall see in Chapter 3, this has the potential to compromise any subsequent findings in evidential terms.

The officers dealing with the scene will try to seal off as large an area as possible so as to safeguard the integrity of any subsequent finds. A good example of how far police will go was demonstrated in the shooting of Gerry Tobin on the M40 in August 2007, when Thames Valley Police closed the whole motorway so that they could search for evidence. The key point to remember is that, from an *evidential* point of view, there is only one chance to examine the scene. Once it has been released and can be visited by anyone outside of the investigation the evidential value of anything then found is almost zero, although it may have a high *intelligence* value. An example of the difference between these two classifications would be where a fingerprint is found in a car that has been used during the crime. It has little evidential value on its own as there is no way of knowing when and where the contact took place, but it can be extremely valuable intelligence in identifying a potential suspect. It becomes of evidential value if the owner of the print denies having ever been in the car.

Having established a perimeter the next two tasks are to set out a corridor for entry and exit, and to begin a log recording who has visited the scene and when. At this point, unless there is the opportunity to pursue a named suspect, the uniformed officers' task is complete and CID will take charge of the scene. A final couple of points from a writer's point of view: the average uniformed constable, and certainly the Duty Officer, will have seen more dead bodies, in more extreme conditions of dismemberment and putrefaction than their CID counterparts, as they deal regularly with road traffic accidents and people who are found weeks after they have died. They are thus less likely to feel the need to throw up at the scene. Secondly, it is rarely the sight of a body, regardless of its state, that causes people to gag; it is always the smell. It seems to get into the very mucous of the nose and stays there for some time, regardless of masks or copious amounts of perfume or aftershave.

The Detectives

The rank of the first detective to attend the scene will depend on the time of day. During office hours it will probably be a detective inspector (DI) or a detective chief inspector (DCI). From 7 p.m. to 8 a.m. it will either be a detective sergeant (DS) or a detective constable (DC); the former is more likely in a large town a city, the latter in a rural location. Having surveyed the scene of the crime the decision will be made, either by the officer if they are sufficiently senior (DCI), or in consultation with a senior officer, on the scale of effort the investigation will require. A straightforward domestic killing may be handled by a DS and a small team of DCs working in the general office, but a complicated 'stranger' killing will require a large team working out of a dedicated incident room. When you consider that in the series of attacks on prostitutes that took place around Ipswich in December 2006 Suffolk were assisted in both the patrol and detective functions by all the surrounding forces and by the Metropolitan Police, it makes some fiction, where the team is a man, a woman and a dog, look more than a little incredible. In every case a Senior Investigating Officer (SIO) will be appointed, usually a detective superintendent or a DCI. In a domestic murder their role will be overall supervision, with little personal input. In a complex murder they will be dedicated solely to the investigation.

The Crime Scene

Once the crime scene is secured it is important that access is controlled and that people attend, as far as possible, in the right order. The first person to arrive after the police, is usually the Divisional Surgeon, who will declare life extinct. This is done even in cases where the person is very obviously dead as it is not unknown for defence counsel to raise it as an issue at trial. The next person is the photographer as it is important to try to capture the scene before it is disturbed, and to photograph the body from as many angles as possible before it is removed. A video recording will also be made, which significantly aids in briefing those who have not attended the scene and in showing the jury a more complete picture of the crime scene. The need to preserve the scene from contamination by any DNA traces now means that even the SIO will avoid disturbing things if at all possible. A camera has been developed which can take a picture of the scene 'in the round' to help in this. If the killing is in any way complicated and there is a likelihood that attending the scene will be helpful in the post-mortem, the pathologist will be asked to attend. This does not occur routinely, however, because of a number of factors: the availability of the pathologist, the need to remove the body, etc. After this the scene is left to the Scenes of Crimes Officers (SOCOs) to capture all of the forensic evidence available.

As much as possible will be done leaving the body *in situ*. If it is indoors this is relatively straightforward; outside and in a public place it becomes more difficult. In recent years it has become common practice to erect a tent over the immediate scene, both to screen the body from public view and to preserve the scene for as long as possible. Writers should be aware of the fact that practices in preserving the scene, allowing access and general levels of professionalism have changed significantly in the last twenty to thirty years. It used to be common practice, especially in the smaller county forces, for senior officers to attend and trample all over the scene, whether or not they were part of the investigation, and for very little to be done to preserve it except in the immediate vicinity of the body. Current practice is that:

- only those involved in the investigation attend the scene
- access be kept to a minimum
- those accessing the scene wear protective clothing
- as large an area around the body be preserved for examination as is practicable.

The recurring theme is the need to preserve the evidential integrity of anything found.

The forensic examination of the scene is essentially looking for:

- anything missing that one would expect to find there
- anything at the scene which is foreign to it
- samples of all blood and body fluids at the scene
- anything which may have DNA traces, such as a cigarette end
- all fingerprints for comparison and elimination
- any other physical marks such as tool marks where there is a break-in, footprints or tyre tracks.

The Incident Room

The complexity of a murder investigation is such that most SIOs prefer, as far as possible, to staff the incident room with people they know and whose judgement they can rely on. Most of the work is now assisted by computerization through the HOLMES system. The team is usually housed in a room or suite of rooms which most larger stations have dedicated specifically for this purpose.

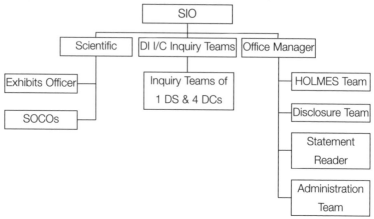

Figure 1: Murder Enquiry Structure

The SIO

The SIO can be either a detective superintendent or a DCI. The preference is for superintendent, as this rank has additional powers to search and take intimate samples, thus making the enquiry team more self-sufficient. All SIOs have been specifically trained in the task and in larger forces only selected superintendents will carry out the role. In smaller forces it is essential that every detective superintendent is able to carry out this function efficiently. As in most fiction the SIO will inevitably have a 'bagman', someone to act as their 'gopher' and dogsbody. This will normally be a detective sergeant (DS).

The SIO is responsible for the overall management of the case and specifically for deciding which lines of inquiry will be pursued and how this will be done. It is vital that they keep an open mind, as the cases of Colin Stagg and Jeremy Bamber show (see Chapter 4). All of this is logged in the Policy Book. This means that:

- the lines of enquiry can be audited
- anyone joining the investigation can quickly get up to speed on how it has been developed and why some lines of inquiry are being pursued and others not
- the review process, which takes place routinely if there is no arrest, can look at the decisions made in the context of the time and state of knowledge of the SIO when they were made. This makes it easier to understand the thinking of the SIO and minimizes the effect of hindsight.

The Office Manager

This officer is responsible for running the Incident Room. He or she can be either a DI or a DS. Skill and experience are more important than rank and most SIOs prefer to work with officers that they know and trust as this is a key post. If done efficiently it frees the SIO to focus on the inquiry itself rather than the management of the incident room.

Everything that the SIO or Statement Reader (see later) requires to be done is noted in the Action Book. This is a simple book of duplicate pages, one of which is detachable. Each task is entered in the book, with details of exactly what needs to be done, who should do it and when it should be done by. The top copy is detached from the book and given to the inquiry team. A key role of the Incident Room Manager is to chase up on the progress of these actions, ensuring that they are all completed on time and that nothing is missed. When the action is completed the top copy is returned and the Incident Room Manager decides whether all actions are complete or more must be done on any particular line of inquiry. The system has been computerized through the HOLMES system but for some time most SIOs preferred to stick to the paper system partly because it was tried and tested, and partly because the management team did not have the computer skills to enter the information directly. In addition a book is easier to access and cannot crash. Even now a paper copy is kept of the actions for the same reasons.

The importance of the role of the Office Manager cannot be overstated. Most difficult inquiries lead to the accumulation of massive amounts of information, most of which is irrelevant. The key tasks are:

- to control the flow of the information
- to ensure that all of the tasks identified are carried out
- to spot coincidences or inconsistencies which need to be followed up.

Most murders are cleared up by the dogged perseverance of the detectives in patiently following up every lead and, by process of elimination, ending up with a prime suspect on whom they can then focus. For this to work it is essential that the system can manage the information so that as detectives go out every day they are up to date on the results of the inquiries made by the other teams.

The Statement Reader

Before HOLMES the Statement Reader was the centre of the inquiry process. He or she reads every statement coming in, either from the teams or obtained from outside forces in order to ensure that every 'i' has been dotted and every 't' crossed. If they are not satisfied they instigate another 'action' for further work to be done. In addition, they will also mark up the statement with all the items to be indexed on the HOLMES system. This gives them a unique view of the whole enquiry; their brain is the first and, some would argue, the best computer used in murder investigations.

HOLMES

In the 1980s the Home Office identified that computerization could greatly assist major inquiries where large amounts of information were accumulated and where paper-based indexing systems, and the computer that is the Statement Reader's brain, could no longer cope with the volume. They developed an approach which was given the name HOLMES, the acronym being developed, somewhat laboriously, from Home Office Large and Major Enquiry System. In order to stimulate competition they left it to the market to provide the computer solution and several companies became involved in developing software and systems. Since they all came to the market at different times, with different specifications and at different costs, forces ended up buying from several suppliers.

To paraphrase Mark Twain, there are liars, damned liars and computer salespeople. Despite assurances from the industry that all the systems could be made compatible, the reality was that none of them could talk to one another nor could there be any electronic exchange of information. The only way that linked inquiries could work where forces had different makes of computer was to set up physical links between incident rooms, with all the information being input as many times as there were systems if cross-referencing was to be possible. This made it clumsy, expensive, time-consuming and very frustrating; thus investigators were reluctant to use the system universally for some considerable time. It was yet another instance where the Home Office confused cost with value for money.

It is only in relatively recent times that the systems have been made compatible and it has been possible to exchange information on a single input basis. HOLMES is now highly developed. All the information gathered in the course of the investigation is input as either evidence (statements, exhibits etc.) or as intelligence. It allows for very sophisticated searches, and if the Statement Reader and indexers have done their work properly, patterns, coincidences and inconsistencies can be identified quickly. It is also far less likely that the mistakes that were made in the Yorkshire Ripper case (when, for example, Sutcliffe was arrested more than once) could occur without alarm bells ringing. There is no doubt that HOLMES has made management of large inquiries much simpler, especially where they involve incidents in more than one force area.

Inquiry Teams

When the body of the victim is found relatively soon after death the first twenty-four to forty-eight hours of the inquiry become vitally important, as it is possible to find witnesses with a clear memory of events inside this time period, and if the suspect can be identified and arrested it is more likely that forensic evidence linking them with the victim or the scene will be found. This means that the SIO will deploy as many officers as possible, both uniformed and CID, at the beginning of the investigation in order to carry out house-to-house inquiries and to position teams where passers-by may have seen something. An essential element of the SIO's job in this period is keeping up to date with the information coming in and ensuring that everyone is briefed on it. After that time the staffing is significantly reduced. It will usually consist of a DI running anywhere between three and five teams of one DS and four DCs. The DCs will usually work in pairs. At first sight this looks like a waste of manpower but experience has shown that it is better to have one officer asking questions whilst the other observes and makes notes and it does make any arrest much safer.

The Family Liaison Officer

In every case of violent or unexplained death a family liaison officer will be appointed to look after the needs of the family *vis-à-vis* the investigation. The duties of this officer are:

- to assess the family in its wider context so as to keep the SIO informed of its needs
- to ensure that the media strategies of the police and the family are co-ordinated so that the public do not get a mixed message
- to get whatever intelligence is possible from the family and family friends
- to look after the interests of the investigation
- to keep a log of all contacts and interactions with the family and family friends.

When the killer is someone from outside the family this job is relatively straightforward as the process is mainly one way, keeping the family informed of the progress of the investigation. When the killer is someone from within the family the situation is significantly more complicated, especially during the period when the person is only a suspect and no arrest has been made. In these cases the liaison officer needs to do exactly the opposite of the job description. It is imperative that they always keep to the front of their mind the fact that they are detectives and investigators first and liaison officers second, so they must gauge what the family can be told without hindering the investigation in any way. In complicated and difficult cases the SIO may deliberately not inform the liaison officer of certain facts so that the latter can be open with the family. This is not always possible as the officer needs to be well informed if they are to carry out their role as an investigator. It does not need too much imagination to see the stresses that this can cause to the officer, especially if in the course of a long inquiry they form any sort of emotional attachment to members of the family, such as the victim's parents. If the killer is a member of the family this may mean that the liaison officer has to be changed after an arrest, as the arrest will certainly undermine the trust that they have built up with the family.

The Scientific Services Manager

Up until the 1970s, all the forensic functions in most forces were carried out by police officers who had had additional training. From that point on the job itself became more and more skilled and required more and more of a scientific background, especially in the recovery of fingerprints. The increasing use of DNA sampling has significantly accelerated the process and it is now common for most forces to have a separate and distinct function for the maintenance and development of forensic science. In addition, forensic analysis does not come cheap and it has become essential for forces to be able to control the amount of work contracted out to the forensic science service by filtering applications for the examination of exhibits through someone with expert knowledge.

In the initial stages of the investigation the forensic team leads the way. It is unusual to have witnesses who can name or point to possible suspects. It is certain that the suspect, once arrested, will deny the charge so it is essential that evidence is found which will link him or her with the scene and with the victim. Once all the forensic evidence is recovered the forensic scientists fade into the background and only re-emerge when a suspect comes into the frame and needs to be either charged or eliminated. Those writers who wish to develop a storyline or plot in which forensic evidence plays a central part should be aware of the fact that this is an area which is developing quickly and which is highly technical, as in the use of DNA when a very small sample has been recovered. I will cover this and give some background on the evidential difficulties that it presents in Chapter 3. Tempting though it may be, an extensive knowledge of the storylines in television shows such as *CSI* and *Silent Witness* is not adequate background on which to base a plot (indeed some of the scriptwriters and their advisors would benefit from reading this book!). The writer needs to research the issue using materials as up to date as he or she can acquire and understand (or persuade someone with that knowledge to brief them).

The Exhibits Officer

In every inquiry the police seize physical evidence which links the criminal to the crime or which is evidence that the crime has been committed. In 'stranger' murders where there is a complicated crime scene there can be a very large volume of seized material. To understand the difficulty that this presents it is necessary to understand the legal concept known as the 'chain of evidence'. Put simply this means that the prosecution must be able to show that any item they present in evidence was actually that which was taken from the scene. There needs to be an auditable paper trail which confirms how it was conveyed to the police station, then to the place where the forensic analysis took place and then back into police custody for presentation by the prosecution in court as an exhibit. In order to ensure that nothing goes wrong in this process every enquiry will have its Exhibits Officer. They will have responsibility for:

- bagging and labelling all exhibits
- making sure that the packaging is correct and will not lead to any deterioration of the exhibit itself, e.g. making sure that bloodied clothing is not put in an airtight container, and that it is stored properly
- that the item is conveyed and recovered properly from the forensic science service
- that the item presented in court can be guaranteed to be the one that was recovered from the scene.

This officer needs to be an obsessive, nit-picking 'finisher' if the SIO is to avoid being ambushed at crown court by either a failure in the chain of evidence or an allegation that the exhibit has been contaminated in some way. It is a particularly onerous and always underrated task, but given both its critical nature and its ability to attract idiosyncratic characters it is one which is worthy of consideration by any crime writer for background colour.

The Disclosure Team

Up until 1996 the only disclosure that the prosecution had to make to the defence was either evidence which they themselves intended to introduce in the trial or evidence which they had come across and which they judged would be helpful to the defence. There were a number of cases in which it was found on appeal that the prosecution had knowledge of issues which were either helpful to the defence or could potentially undermine the prosecution case, where the defence had been kept in ignorance of them.

As a result the Criminal Procedures and Investigation Act 1996 introduced a duty on the prosecution to disclose all evidence to the defence other than that which they thought held some degree of privilege, such as the use and identity of informants. This duty of disclosure has been reduced by the Criminal Justice Act 2003 but the volume of information handled by any murder inquiry is such that it is still necessary to have a number of officers reviewing it as it comes in and deciding what should be disclosed to the defence. It has been found to be more efficient to do this as the inquiry progresses rather than waiting until someone is arrested and charged. It does not need much imagination to realize the tensions that this can produce where an arrest has been made but the SIO is not certain that all of the participants have been identified. In addition it is a bit like expecting a turkey to vote for Christmas to ask an SIO to bring an objective mind to bear on disclosing evidence to the defence which is not directly helpful to their case but does have the potential to undermine that of the prosecution.

Lines of Approach

The difficulty representing a real-life inquiry presents to the writer is that the murder will usually occur very early on in the book, probably just at the point where the writer is trying to establish the main characters in the mind of the reader. To do this successfully most teachers/editors/publishers advise that the number of people used in the opening chapters is kept to a minimum. This seems to discourage even established writers from describing the inquiry team and the incident room. In my view this is misguided as they can provide wonderful background colour. For example Ian Rankin succeeds because he is so good at immersing the reader in the atmosphere of the police station and the police culture. If you can get a handle on the chatter, joking and repartee that takes place when a group of men and women are brought together in these circumstances it will give the opening chapters, and thus the book, a powerful atmosphere. An example of the sort of black humour that could be used comes from a multiple murder in Tooting, London. There had been a long-running dispute between two families – one Irish, one English – which boiled over into a long and bloody fight in which one Irishman and three Englishmen were killed. The briefing board was headed 'England 1 – Ireland 3' – at least until the SIO ordered it wiped clean.

The briefings can be used to develop the plot, lay down red herrings and show aspects of the protagonist through short, sharp interchanges with officers at the briefing who need not play any future part in the story. In much the same way the bureaucracy, the need to manage the overtime budget, the frustration of not getting enough staff, or the wrong people, can all be used to develop tension between the protagonist and the senior officers or the team, or to give reasons why lines of inquiry which later proved to be fruitful were not initially pursued.

CHAPTER 2

The Tools of the Trade

Every occupation has its tools of the trade and these are the ones used by the police. If they haven't got the powers they need then they have always been very good at falling back on bluff.

Background

The history of police powers to stop, search and arrest is like a potted history of social development in the nineteenth and twentieth centuries. Before the nineteenth century London was the only large city in England; most of the population lived in small towns and villages. Everyone knew everyone else and strangers stood out, automatically raising suspicions if they were poor. Every subject had a duty under the common law to join in the 'hue and cry'. Powers to detain were very limited, much more a matter of might than right; the only real constraint was the law of habeas corpus, the requirement that anyone detaining someone else had to justify it to a judge if called upon to do so, a core concept of English law but at the time really only available to the wealthy or the well connected.

Things began to change in the nineteenth century. Britain had been more or less continually at war with France until 1815. After every major war there was always the serious problem of dealing with the soldiers and sailors, many mutilated or crippled, who had been summarily discharged back into the community, usually flooding the labour market at a time of low demand. The Napoleonic Wars were no exception to this and in the 1820s England was infested with 'rogues and vagabonds' wandering the countryside, surviving by begging and stealing. The Vagrancy Act 1824, a very early example of 'nimbyism', gave local constables and magistrates extensive powers to ensure that these poor souls moved on to someone else's patch (and Poor Law provision) on pain of being arrested and locked up. Then came the establishment of the Metropolitan Police in 1829. That force was given what were then seen as extensive powers to stop, search and arrest under the Metropolitan Police Act 1839. The combination of the Vagrancy Act and this Act gave rise to the notorious 'sus' issues of the 1970s and 1980s; the Metropolitan Police Act gave police powers to stop and search persons reasonably suspected of carrying stolen goods and the Vagrancy Act created the offence of 'being a suspected person loitering to commit a felony [later 'an arrestable offence']', one of the very few provisions in English law where the *suspected* intention to commit a crime, evidenced by an act that was less than an attempt, was enough to create criminal liability.

For any crime writer who would like to consider mixing the genre with history this is an era well worth considering. Society was in the midst of massive change as it became industrialized and urbanized. The ruling classes were still worried that the effects of the two revolutions, the American and French, would spread to Britain, a fear compounded by the demands of the Chartists for democratic reform. There was no standing army and the imposition of order depended on an unreliable mixture of the magistracy, such local government as existed, the local militia and volunteer constables. The ineffectiveness of these arrangements is well demonstrated by what happened in Bristol in 1831, when the mayor and colonel of the militia were imprisoned for failing to put down a mob which went on to burn out a large section of the city.

There were more firearms and deadly weapons around than today. The war had led to large amounts being manufactured and every gentleman, and many who thought themselves such, felt entitled to carry a sword and a pistol, especially when travelling. Such police as existed outside London would be armed with pistol and cutlass as a matter of routine, especially if patrolling at night; and of course, in the absence of any professional detectives (the CID was not properly established in the Met until the 1860s), there was more scope for amateurs to become legitimately involved in crime detection.

As the nineteenth century progressed Britain rapidly changed from being a rural, quasi-feudal society into an urbanized, industrial one. The social and legislative developments ran in parallel with that change. By the 1890s every community had its own police force (albeit of very variable quality) and much of the criminal common law had been codified into statute. In the course of doing this each Act created its own particular police powers of stop, search and arrest. When I joined the police in 1970 the state of the law was such that a major part of police training was the rote learning of a whole compendium of powers, each with its own particular limitations. A power of arrest for 'misdemeanours', for example, could only be used between the hours of 9 p.m. and 6 a.m., and a multiplicity of powers of arrest could only be carried out by an officer – sometimes in uniform, sometimes not – where he or she found the offender committing the offence.

In the late 1960s, Roy Jenkins, almost certainly the greatest reforming Home Secretary, set up the Law Commission to reform and codify the law. Its recommendations concerning police powers of arrest were enacted in the Criminal Law Act 1967. This created 'arrestable offences' (serious offences for which you could be imprisoned for five years or more) and greatly simplified and extended police powers of arrest. In 2005 the powers were further simplified and extended by the Serious and Organized Crime Act 2005. The power of arrest created by this Act is such that only a very stupid or very unimaginative police officer would not be able to interpret the circumstances before him or her so as to warrant arrest.

Stop and search however remained a dog's dinner until the Police and Criminal Evidence Act 1984 (PACE). The difficulties faced by the police are exemplified by the fact that until 1984 people could be searched for drugs and stolen goods but not for weapons, and a search warrant could be obtained for just about anything except to find a body where murder was suspected! This latter circumstance gave rise to a comment which aptly demonstrates the attitude of both the judiciary and politicians towards the police in terms of carrying out their duties despite rather than with the assistance of the law. In *Ghanni v. Jones*, a case of suspected murder where the police could not find the body and the law did not provide for a search warrant to be issued in the circumstances, Lord Denning said:

The police have to get the permission of the house-holder to enter if they can; or, if not, do it by stealth or by force. Somehow they seem to manage. No decent person refuses them permission. If he does he is prob-ably implicated in some way or other. So the police risk an action for trespass. It is not much risk.

In other words it is acceptable to the police not just to find a way around the law but to actually break it provided it is for the greater good. The same situation applied until 2000 concerning bugging the houses of major criminals and terrorists where police had to commit criminal acts (damage) and civil torts (trespass) in order to get the job done simply because politicians found the issue too hot to handle.

Powers to stop and search were codified and rational-ized by PACE so that in essence officers can carry out a search if they reasonably suspect that a person has articles unlawfully obtained or is carrying an offensive weapon. These powers have been massively extended by the Terrorism Acts (too many to cover in detail), where a person may be stopped and searched in any 'designated area' if the officer believes it is expedient in the prevention of acts of terrorism – reasonable suspicion is no longer needed.

In summary, from a writer's point of view, police after 1984 have general powers of stop, search and arrest based on reasonable suspicion in terms of the general law and extensive powers in designated areas where acts of terrorism are anticipated after 2000. The rate of change in anti-terrorism legislation is such that anyone writing on the issue is advised to carry out specific research at the time of writing if they believe that accuracy on this point is essential to the plot.

34

Stop and Search

The power to stop and search on reasonable suspicion is one of the most powerful preventive and detective weapons in the police armoury. A significant number of major criminals, including the Black Panther and the Yorkshire Ripper, were detected and arrested by uniformed patrol officers using this power, initially because they 'didn't like the look of them'. Today forces try to make best use of patrol by developing intelligence packages focused on target criminals. These are people with a known criminal record the police suspect of being currently active. Patrol officers then check them out on sight in order to identify:

- any vehicles they are using or have access to
- their associates
- where they are currently living
- current girlfriends (the targets are usually male and girlfriends/wives make excellent informants, usually for reasons of revenge)
- whether they have money or are broke.

If a target comes into the frame in an inquiry the investigator then has a head-start on some of his movements, transport, possible informants etc.

This information used to be kept in a card index system by someone called the Collator, now the Local Intelligence Officer (LIO). Nowadays forces have computerized systems and filtration processes to ensure that the information input is verified and politically correct – entries on the card system often had much greater entertainment than intelligence value.

The use of this power leads to the 'catch 22' of profiling.

An analysis of crimes will often lead to the conclusion that a particular section of the (usually young male) population is engaged in a particular crime (e.g. young whites in car theft, young blacks in street robbery). The briefing to officers in these circumstances must make it clear that, as well as matching the profile, the person stopped and searched must have done something which gives the officer reasonable suspicion that he is in possession of something (such as drugs or a weapon) illegally. As far as terrorism is concerned the need for reasonable suspicion disappears and it is much more likely that people will be stopped, questioned and searched merely on the basis of the profile, thus further alienating the very people who may be able to provide intelligence and support.

The power to stop and search is regulated by Code of Practice A of PACE. In essence this requires that:

- police action (other than in the case of terrorism) be based on reasonable suspicion
- the person be treated with as much dignity as is possible in the circumstances
- the person be given reasons for the stop before any search is carried out
- a written record of the reasons be given when the search is completed.

This also applies to 'field interrogations' – stop and question – although both the main political parties are now calling for this requirement to be dropped. Throughout my career I have been struck by the irony of the fact that every call by politicians that the police be freed from bureaucracy is always matched by those same politicians requiring, in knee-jerk response to an incident, that more and more information be formally recorded in order to cover their backs. I have no doubt that the current review being carried out by Sir Ronnie Flanagan will lead to the same outcome.

Fruit of the Poisoned Tree

It is worth dealing here with the issue of evidence which the police have obtained illegally – for example as a result of a search for which there was no adequate reason or no power. The term for this is 'fruit of the poisoned tree'. Although English and US criminal law are both based on the English Common Law, practice in England is profoundly different from that in the USA. There, the citizen's rights under its written constitution have led the courts to rule that any evidence which has not been obtained following 'due process' will be ruled inadmissible. This is now so firmly established that the District Attorney will not even try to argue it in, no matter how critical it is to the issue of guilt.

In England and Wales this is not the case. Evidence is considered on its own merits and the issue of how it was obtained is usually regarded as irrelevant. The defence will inevitably try to have it ruled inadmissible but they are almost always unsuccessful. The more critical the issue is to proving the case against the defendant, the less likely it is that it will be found to be inadmissible. The major exception to this is where a person is induced by a police officer to commit a crime. If the court considers that the crime would not have been committed had the officer not encouraged or induced the defendant, then it will acquit. An example of this is a drugs buy. It is appropriate for an officer to approach someone suspected of being a trafficker and offer to buy. On the other hand if the officer induces someone who is not already engaged in trafficking to obtain drugs, the court will almost certainly take the view that the crime would not have been committed had the officer not prompted it and the defendant will be acquitted.

Arrest and Detention

The most straightforward way of thinking through the arrest process is to see it as one of escalation of police interest as follows:

witness	someone who can provide either evidence about, or intelligence which may lead to identifying, an offender
general suspect	someone who cannot be eliminated from the inquiry at this time (as you can see, this is a negative test as the investigator will want to keep all options open)
specific suspect	someone against whom there is some evidence, albeit weak, but whom it is worthwhile either investigating further or eliminating
detained suspect	someone against whom there is significant evidence and whom it is worth arresting so as to interrogate them and search their home, place of work etc. for forensic or documentary evidence (this will often be an associate of the actual offender who on questioning informs on them to save their own neck)
charged prisoner	someone against whom there is enough evidence to make a conviction likely and whom the police would prefer to keep in custody while they pursue their final inquiries.

A person may move in and out of the first four categories as the evidence available to the investigator changes. Under PACE a person may only be detained for a limited time before being charged (see below) and it is now common practice for police to develop as much of the case as possible before arrest as long as the investigator is confident that the suspect is unlikely to make a bolt for it.

Before 1984 police could detain suspects without charge for up to five days. This came as a shock to my law lecturer when I read law in 1975. He thought, as did most of the legal profession not engaged in the criminal law, that they could only detain for up to twenty-four hours. At that time the issue was governed by the Magistrates Court Act which stated that the suspect should be charged and brought before the court 'as soon as is practicable'. In serious cases dealing with professional criminals (at that time usually armed robbers or gangsters working vice and extortion rackets) the practice was to arrest the gangster and leave him to 'sweat' for a couple of days. On the second or third day his family and friends would find out that he was in police custody and would try to locate him. He would usually be questioned on the third day. Since he had been held incommunicado the suspect had no idea who else had been arrested or what they might have said so was often anxious to ensure that he did not carry the can alone (the 'prisoner's dilemma' – say nothing and hope everyone else does, or get in first and do a deal). By day four the family had usually instructed a solicitor who would be denied access as a matter of routine. On day five the solicitor would apply to the court for a writ of habeas corpus which meant that the police had to justify the detention to the court. At this point there was usually enough evidence to charge the prisoner with something.

All that changed with PACE and its codes of practice.

The Act and its codes are quite technical, very repetitive and thus very boring. They were intended to put suspects back where everyone thought they had been all along and codified what was recognized as best practice. For the writer, the essence is:

- A person can only be detained by police without charge for up to thirty-six hours; the first twenty-four on the authority of an inspector, the remaining twelve on the authority of a superintendent
- The police can apply to a magistrate for further detention of three days. This is relatively rare and police must show solid grounds for it. In most cases it is done with the co-operation of the suspect, often where extensive searches are necessary, such as to find a body
- Anyone detained must be able to tell someone that they have been detained and must be given access to a solicitor and legal advice as soon as they are detained unless there are pressing reasons for not doing so. Access can be denied if a superintendent has reasonable grounds to believe that it would:
  - (i) lead to: interference with, or harm to, evidence connected with an indictable offence, or interference with, or physical harm to, other people
  - (ii) lead to alerting other people suspected of having committed an indictable offence but not yet arrested for it
  - (iii) hinder the recovery of property obtained in consequence of the commission of such an offence.
- A detainee must be given access to the codes of practice and writing materials
- If the suspect is disadvantaged in any way through physical or mental handicap, before they can be interviewed steps must be taken to balance the handicap,

such as by providing an interpreter or ensuring that they are accompanied by a responsible adult who can safeguard their interests

- Juveniles must be accompanied by a responsible adult while they are interviewed
- Searches can only be made by members of the same sex and any strip search must be limited to the removal of clothing. Any attempt to look in any body orifice (e.g. for drugs) is defined as an intimate search which needs the authority of an inspector and must be carried out by a medical practitioner
- If an interview is carried out disregarding the safeguards it will probably be rendered inadmissible.

The Caution

Until 1994 no 'adverse inference' could be drawn from a suspect's refusal to answer questions, even if they were directed at issues about which the suspect had unique or sole knowledge. This left the suspect free to concoct a story later that fitted the facts known to the police. The only exception to this was alibi, an assertion that they were somewhere else at the time of the offence. Notice of this had to be given to the prosecution so that it could be tested before the trial began. Now the suspect no longer has an unbridled right to silence and the prosecution can point out at any subsequent trial that the defendant had had an opportunity to put their case at the time of their arrest but that they did not take it up and that they can draw any inferences or conclusions from that failure. The wording of the caution now is, 'You do not have to say anything. But it may harm your defence if you do not mention when questioned something which you later rely on in court.

Anything you do say may be given in evidence.'

A suspect must be cautioned as soon as the police officer has 'grounds to suspect [him/her] of an offence'. Failure to do so when there are reasonable grounds for suspicion can make anything the suspect then says liable to be ruled inadmissible. This creates a number of interesting scenarios for the crime writer:

- If the investigator has reasonable grounds but for tactical reasons does not want to disclose them (a situation that occurs all too often in real life) there is the tension created by the risk that the suspect says something useful but then clams up once cautioned, considerably reducing the value of the admission
- The investigator may only want intelligence, and rely on that to lead to more substantial evidence, such as knowledge of where a weapon can be found
- The investigator may be willing to risk it in the hope that once a suspect has made an admission they will not be able to go back on it (emotionally they may be relieved to have got it out). This happens surprisingly often in real life but rarely if a lawyer is present.

There is a concept of 'helping police with their inquiries', when someone stays for an extended time at the station answering questions. The key issue is that he or she must be doing so voluntarily. It often happens with some minor player who is hoping that co-operation will mean that their part in the crime will not be pursued. The test of whether or not someone is 'under arrest' does not depend on some formulaic use of words. It depends on the mind of the investigator. If at any point during a 'voluntary' interview the investigator stops the interviewee leaving the room then that person is under arrest from that point on, whether or not anything is said. When this is combined with the fact that a person can only be detained for a limited amount of time it is easy to see how important this issue is for investigators. For that reason the investigator will formally arrest a suspect, sometimes mid-interview, in order to ensure that the courts do not explore this point and rule that the moment of arrest occurred earlier. This can be very important where the interview takes place after a suspect has responded to bail. If someone has been arrested and interviewed on an earlier occasion and detained for say six hours, if they are rearrested the investigator only has eighteen hours left.

There are two other reasons for making the arrest formally. First, it really does take people's breath away, especially if they are not professional criminals, and are otherwise respectable members of the community – the more respectable, the more of a shock. This can lead them into saying or doing things in the heat of the moment which are useful to the investigator's case. Secondly, it gives the investigator control. A formal arrest will always be accompanied by physically taking control, e.g. by taking the person by the arm. Again psychologically this works for the investigator even with hardened criminals, although I hope that we do not in time develop the US pattern of routinely putting everybody in handcuffs and chains.

Searching Premises After Arrest

Every time a celebrity, senior government official or politician is arrested at home in a dawn raid there is an uproar in the press and questions asked about the outrageous way the police have acted, usually accompanied by the comment that they could have just asked them to come to the station – being respectable members of the community they would have complied. The outrage conveniently ignores the fact that these people have been arrested because they are suspected of committing a criminal offence and the police have enough evidence to support the arrest. The police response is inevitably either to remain silent or to say that they have used standard operating procedures. The 'dawn raid' is standard police practice and experience over the years has proved it to be very effective – that is why they do it.

Arresting someone at home or at their place of work is an effective tactic, as it brings with it a number of ancillary advantages. The arrest invariably surprises the suspect, and when people are off balance they say things they other-wise might not. The arrest gives the investigator control of the interview process, where and when it will happen and how long the suspect will be kept in custody. There is also a power under PACE to search the premises where the arrest is made, making it less likely that the suspect can get rid of any incriminating evidence. An invitation to attend the police station not only removes these advantages, it tells the person that he or she is a suspect and what he or she is suspected of. About the only thing it does not do is give the suspect a list of the evidence that the police hope to find on the premises.

Once someone is arrested an inspector can authorize the search of other premises related to the suspect. If necessary this can all be prepared in advance so that the searches are carried out very soon after arrest without the need to get a search warrant. These powers are particularly important where the police suspect that evidence is stored on comput-ers, as is the case with terrorism, paedophilia or obstruction of justice. In these cases it is vital that the computers are seized before the suspect has a chance to wipe, corrupt or destroy the hard disc. It is harder than people think to completely wipe a file off the disc. Even if it is deleted and then deleted from the 'deleted files' file, the information is usually still on the disc and can be recovered by an expert or an expert system.

The Interview

I use this word, as it is the one used in the PACE codes of practice, but from the viewpoint of the participants a better word would be interrogation. Interview implies a meeting of equals with some joint purpose. Interrogation makes it clear that one party is questioning the other to find out what he or she knows. This describes the police purpose with everyone from friendly witness to hostile suspect – to find out what they know or what they are willing to lie about. Most interrogations now take place in the presence of a lawyer and a tape recorder.

Contrary to myth, tape recording was welcomed by the majority of police officers. It is quicker and more accurate than notes and allows the questioner to move matters on at a pace that gives the suspect less opportunity to realize where the interrogation is going. Most police officers would have preferred to have gone straight to videoing the interview but this was resisted by lawyers, partly because it would have meant that they would have had to watch the full interview – they prefer reading a transcript or part of the transcript as it saves them time – and partly because defence lawyers did not like the fact that juries would see the manner and attitude of the suspect, not just hear the words. A 'no comment' said with a sneer and a knowing smile would be interpreted very differently from one accompanied by a nervous twitch in the direction of the accompanying lawyer.

The Role of the Lawyer

The lawyer's job in the interview is to advise the suspect on how to reply to questions; what he or she cannot do is answer the questions on the suspect's behalf. If a lawyer persists in doing this he or she can be excluded, although the suspect should be offered the opportunity to consult another lawyer before the interview can proceed.

Now that the prosecution can make use of the fact that the defendant failed to answer questions the investigator may want to put questions to the suspect even if it is likely that there will be no comment, as the failure to answer can become a part of the case against him or her. But they can only go so far in this. They cannot do a Paxman and ask the same question nineteen times, nor can they continue to ask questions if it may be considered oppressive or if the prejudicial effect of a failure to answer outweighs its evidential value.

In a surprising number of cases the outcome desired by both the police officer and the lawyer will be the same. If there is a strong case against the suspect it is often in their best interests to make a full and frank admission and to take up as little of the court's time as possible with the facts of the case, leaving the lawyer as much room as possible to put forward any mitigation. The court also takes a benevolent view towards prisoners who do not subject their victims to the ordeal of going through the trial process. In writing fiction, however, the lawyer presents a very good opportunity to create tension and conflict. Like any other group in society there are good and bad lawyers with good and bad intentions. Some of the tricks they use to reduce the time the police have to question their clients include:

- deliberately arriving late
- taking an inordinately long time to be briefed by the client
- agreeing to represent more than one of the suspects, so only one can be interviewed at a time.

It has been known for lawyers to be in cahoots with the criminals they represent and to act as conduits for the suspect either to warn other members of the gang or to ensure that steps are taken to dispose of stolen property or evidence. Bent lawyers are a particularly difficult group of people for police to handle, since they are entitled to consult their clients in private and can raise privilege on almost all the documentation in their offices. They are technically 'officers of the court', and judges are reluctant to endorse or authorize action against them. On the other hand, it is necessary to point out that a number of inadequate detectives blame their failures unfairly on the lawyers who are only doing their job in representing their clients effectively.

Most police questioning in real life would be very boring to write about. The officers know what they must prove and take a suspect through all the issues relevant to the offence, usually following a prepared template. A lot of the evidence elicited is essentially negative in nature. For example I once questioned a man arrested for living on immoral earnings (he ran a string of prostitutes working West End clubs) for most of the day. He denied the charge throughout but the purpose of the interview was to show that he had no legal sources of income which could sustain his lifestyle. He lived in a luxury flat in Maida Vale, owned a top-of-the-range Mercedes and had wardrobes full of expensive clothes – all apparently on the £5,000 a year that his minicab firm produced. At the end of the session he thought he had done well in never having admitted the offence. He did not look quite so comfortable at trial, as the interview had effectively cut off any chance of producing any other evidence of income.

The investigator seeks either to close down future defences or to find a lie. One of the best examples I have come across in looking for the lie involved one of the best detectives I have worked with – Roger Hoy, a uniformed sergeant in Dorking, Surrey. We had had a series of night-time garage breaks, where the burglars then set fire to the garages, eliminating any forensics. The gang (we knew from sightings that there were at least three of them) had caused about £250,000 worth of damage. They worked a part of the town that contained very high-value properties. Roger persuaded his team to stake out the area – not easy as it was one of the coldest Februaries I've known. At the end of the first week's stake-out they almost caught the gang but they seemed to go magically to earth.

From this Roger deduced that they lived in the area and he doggedly worked his way around all the houses containing any young men between the ages of eighteen and thirty. At one garage a top for an MG sports car had been stolen so Roger also looked for anyone who owned an MG. Eventually he found a lad who had owned an MG sports car but had sold it. Most people would have given up here, especially since Roger was doing much of the work in his own time, but he persisted. He found the dealer in Croydon to whom the car had been sold and went to see him. The dealer said that he had since sold the car, but on being pushed by Roger he did say that it had had two hoods. Roger then went to see the lad, who worked in a local estate agent, and raised the issue of the car hood. The lad said that he had sold the car with just one hood. The lie. As soon as he was arrested he admitted all the offences and put the other two in the frame. All of them were of previous good character so even if we had had found fingerprints we would have had nothing with which to compare them.

One element in fictional interrogation which is also true to life is the 'good cop, bad cop' routine. It is particularly useful where the suspect has had no experience of police or the criminal process. It is rather a waste of time with professional criminals in terms of producing admissions but it can be useful if the investigator only seeks intelligence, as this may be gained by way of threat or inducement, both of which would be fatal to the evidential value of any admissions made.

There is little doubt that PACE and its developments have meant that the British police are probably the most restricted in the developed world in terms of detention times and questioning techniques. This has arisen out of the fact that the police in England and Wales have developed their processes under the English Common Law without the political influences that are part and parcel of the US approach, or the supervision of the investigating magistrate which is usually part of the continental systems, most of which are based on the Napoleonic Code (see Chapter 10 for more detail). PACE however does not cover everything and it is surprising how effective old techniques are such as putting prisoners in adjoining cells and then listening in on their conversation, or putting a police officer in a cell with the prisoner, posing as another prisoner. These approaches are especially useful in finding intelligence rather than evidence.

When the investigator has sufficient evidence to provide

a realistic prospect of a conviction he must take the prisoner before the custody officer to be formally charged. If the prisoner is suspected of a number of offences the investigator can delay doing this until there is sufficient evidence on all the charges. The timing of the decision to charge is very important as the suspect cannot be questioned after being charged unless the interview is necessary:

- to prevent or minimize harm or loss to some other person, or to the public
- to clear up an ambiguity in a previous answer or statement
- in the interests of justice for the detainee to have put to them, and have opportunity to comment on, information concerning the offence which has come to light since they were charged or informed they might be prosecuted.

Implications for the Writer

By now you will realize that if writers follow all the rules they will write some very turgid prose, full of technical language. Here, as elsewhere, the golden rule is not to get involved in the technicalities unless your story demands it. That said, I think that any crime writer who wishes the story to be credible should bear the following in mind:

- The time that anyone can be detained is very limited so do not keep a suspect locked up for too long
- By all means have the investigator interview the suspect without a lawyer but know that it is unlikely to happen and at least think about providing a good

reason for it, such as arrogance or time constraints
- In real life police will always prefer to interview a suspect at a police station – it's their territory and the threat of possible arrest is much more real
- Some of the provisions of the law can assist the writer in providing tension and conflict. These might include interference of the lawyer, the involvement of the Crown Prosecution Service (CPS), a hysterical parent or a difficult and unco-operative social worker.

CHAPTER 3

Forensics

The police service finds itself completing a full circle as far as the examination of forensic evidence is concerned. Initially forces developed their own expertise or approached experts on a case-by-case basis. This led the Home Office to set up the Forensic Science Service (FSS) which dealt with the needs of the police and other government agencies. In the 1990s the FSS was changed from a government department to a government-owned company and began to charge police forces for every examination that it carried out. This has led to forces developing their own forensic science capability in order to be able to screen exhibits so as to reduce the number which are sent for examination or to be able to carry out the examination themselves so that they can obtain the evidence without any additional cost. Anything complicated will be sent to the FSS, but forces have a growing capability for examining footprints, shoeprints and marks left by tools etc. at the scenes of crime.

Locard's Exchange Principle

Wherever he steps, whatever he touches, whatever he leaves, even unconsciously, will serve as a silent witness against him. Not only his fingerprints or his footprints, but his hair, the fibres from his clothes, the glass he breaks, the tool mark he leaves, the paint he scratches, the blood or semen he deposits or collects. All of these and more, bear mute witness against him. This is evidence that does not forget. It is not confused by the excitement of the moment. It is not absent because human witnesses are. It is factual evidence. Physical evidence cannot be wrong, it cannot perjure itself, it cannot be wholly absent. Only human failure to find it, study and understand it, can diminish its value.

So said Professor Edmond Locard (1877–1966) whose Exchange Principle is the basis of forensic evidence. He created the first crime laboratory in Lyons in 1910 and was the father of forensic science.

Forensic literally means 'used in court'. Forensic evidence has come to mean the physical evidence recovered from a crime scene, a victim or a perpetrator, which links the latter to the crime in some way. Its value lies in the fact that it stands by itself and is objective, so the more interpretation is needed the less useful it is. As we will see this is an important point when considering DNA and blood, and it can now be an issue with fingerprints. Forensic evidence's objectivity means that it is essential that its integrity is sustained. This integrity applies to two elements: the scene and the exhibit. In a murder it is assumed that the last person at the scene was the killer. It is essential that the scene is isolated to minimize the probability that anyone can contaminate it. As far as the exhibit is concerned the prosecution must be able to prove two things: that the piece of evidence which they produced as an exhibit is what they say it is – human hair not animal fur, fibres that match the clothing of the victim, etc.; and that nothing has happened to it between its recovery and its examination which could cause it to be changed or contaminated in any way. As we saw in Chapter 1, to do this they must establish a clear chain of evidence which links the movement of the exhibit from the scene to the lab. Any break in the chain will fundamentally undermine the integrity of the exhibit.

Forensic evidence is only useful if it either links a suspect to the crime in a way that indicates guilt or undermines their credibility. For example, a fingerprint found at the scene of the crime is of no value if the suspect had, and admits to having, access to it. It is only of evidential value if they could not lawfully have been there or if they deny ever having been there. Similarly, with any object found at the scene, the prosecution must be able to show either that it could only have been left there by the perpetrator or that it is highly improbable that anyone else could have left it there. This means that fibres from a suspect's jacket which are found on the clothing of the victim have much more evidential value than those found snagged on a nearby bush. If that bush is on or near a footpath their value is even more diminished. It will increase if the jacket fibre is an unusual one and if the suspect denies ever being anywhere near the scene. The relative value of exhibits is shown graphically in this illustration, known as a Johari Window.

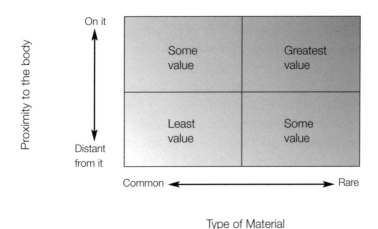

Figure 2: Relative Value of Forensic Material

Fibres and other material from the victim found on the suspect have much more weight and value than the other way around, as common material could have been picked up by the victim anywhere, at any time. If the material is found either on the suspect or in some unusual spot, such as the boot of their car, it has more value.

Forensic evidence is best dealt with in three classifications: exchange materials, fingerprints and body fluids which provide DNA.

Exchange Materials

It is impossible to list all the possible external exchanges that can occur, but those described below are the most common.

Fibres

These are the most common exchange materials in both fact and fiction for the obvious reason that most murders in Britain require contact between the victim and the killer, as the use of firearms is still uncommon. In non-domestic murders there is usually some attempt to hide the body and this again requires some form of contact. Once contact has occurred the only certain way of completely destroying the evidence is the destruction of any material involved – all clothing and any carpeting or lining in a car used to transport the victim, living or dead. Even the most thorough cleaning cannot be relied on to remove all contact material and science is continually developing ways of finding trace materials, such as the use of powders which will attach to contaminants and can then be found by using ultraviolet light to fluoresce them.

Any recovered fibres can be linked in two ways. First they can be analysed and found to be the same material; obviously the rarer the material the more weight it has as evidence. A strand of wool from a Marks and Spencer's cardigan will not have quite the same impact as one from a cashmere sweater sold only through Harrods. Secondly, if the material was cut or broken off in some way it may be possible to make a physical match of the cut or broken ends.

Hair

This is the next most common exchange product. Human beings cast hair all the time and there will always be some sort of exchange in a violent attack. Hair can be matched in the same way as fibres. Analysis can determine whether or not it is human hair or animal fur. If it was cut then a physical match may be possible. DNA analysis is only possible, however, if the root is still attached.

Because it is so fine and difficult to see, hair presents the killer with the same problems as fibre. Rapists have shown an increasing awareness of this in that a significant number of them now meticulously comb and clean the pubic area of the victim, adding significantly to the horror of the attack.

Footprints

This is a growing field for the police, helped by the fact that most young men (who commit most crimes) now wear trainers rather than shoes, and trainer manufacturers continually change their sole patterns as part of their strategy to make their shoes distinctive. The FSS are slowly building up a database, as are a number of forces. Most forces now routinely take the footprints of suspects whom they believe to be active criminals, especially suspected burglars.

The usefulness of a footprint is determined by:

- the rarity of the sole pattern
- the size and clarity of the recovered footprint (it can be very clear if it has moved through fluid and onto a flat surface such as a kitchen floor)
- the age of the shoe – the older the shoe the more likely it is that it has acquired unique marks
- the time between the offence and the arrest of the suspect – the shorter this is the more likely it is that the patterns of damage or wear will match.

In Bedfordshire in 1996 a murder occurred where a footprint was the critical piece of evidence. The victim and her husband were renovating their large, isolated house and during the work were living in a caravan parked in the garden. The woman was attacked when on her own one afternoon and after the assault the killer left her body in the caravan together with a load of straw which he then set fire to. All the caravan windows were closed. When he closed the door on leaving, he deprived the fire of oxygen, causing it to smoulder rather than burn. Some time later a passer-by noticed smoke coming from the caravan and went to investigate. When he opened the door the fire immediately took hold. He managed to drag the woman's body out of the caravan but the van itself was quickly devoured by the fire. This meant that the only source of forensic evidence was what was left of the victim's body and clothing.

The victim had been killed by being stabbed in the throat with a screwdriver. During the assault the killer had at some point stamped on the victim's face several times with considerable force, leaving it marked. The SIO, Detective Superintendent Dave Tomlinson, succeeded in finding a pathologist who could recover the mark as a useable print and it was sent to the FSS but no match was made. When it was returned to Bedford a sharp-eyed SOCO thought it looked similar to one recently taken from an active burglar and the match was made.

Tyre Prints
Like trainers most makes of tyre have distinctive tread patterns which can be helpful in confirming identification once a suspect is brought into the frame. They are usually only useful in helping to find a suspect in the first place if they are very unusual, thus limiting the number of people that the inquiry team need to eliminate. Once a suspect is arrested they can provide strong circumstantial evidence.

Tools and Weapons
The exchange that takes place here is not materials (other

than blood, flesh and hair with weapons) but marks. When tools or weapons are used they will leave the mark of any peculiar wear or damage they have on the object or person they were used on. These marks and those on the tools or weapons can then be matched. The more unusual the wear or damage pattern the easier it is to make a match which a forensic scientist can say is exact.

Paint
The usual source of paint in inquiries is cars, usually involved in hit-and-run cases. It can be used in two ways:

- the analysis can identify the make and model of the car
- samples recovered can be physically matched to scratches or patches on the vehicle itself.

Paint is usually used as part of a screening process; the investigator tries to find everyone who owns the make and model identified and then eliminate them from the inquiry. This is an expensive process and will only be used in a very serious crime, usually murder. In difficult inquiries where there is little to go on this has often created enormous workloads for the inquiry teams. In the Yorkshire Ripper case 5.4 million car numbers were taken and checked; in the case of Robert Black (see Chapter 4) a blue Cortina came into the frame and as a result 20,000 owners of blue Cortinas were traced and interviewed. It can lead to spectacular success as in the case of 'The Fox', Malcolm Fairley. In the summer of 1984 he carried out a series of rapes on the Bedfordshire/Buckinghamshire/ Berkshire borders. Over 200 police officers from different forces were deployed on patrol to catch or at least deter him, without success in either. Eventually tiny fragments of 'harvest yellow' paint from a British Leyland car were found where the rapist had reversed his car into some bushes. When the detectives carrying out the elimination inquiries came to see him, Fairley was actually washing his car. They noticed the scratches and when they searched his other car they found more evidence connecting him with the rapes.

There will be an exchange of materials in any contact. Science now helps us trace and then analyse microscopic amounts of material. As the sample gets smaller it is important to bear two issues in mind. First, the smaller the sample the more scrupulous the SOCO must be in preventing contamination. The rejection of the DNA evidence by the judge in the Omagh bombing case powerfully demonstrates what happens when you get this wrong. This means that the scene of a murder will only be visited by SOCOs in the first instance. Some forces now have a special camera that can take a 360-degree photograph of the scene so that the SIO need never actually enter it. Since it can take two or three days before SOCOs can allow access, this has become more and more important. The second issue is that analysis of the sample requires its physical destruction so the smaller sample the more confident the analyst must be of getting a result as there may not be enough for a second attempt.

Fingerprints
Fingerprints were first used for identification in Persia and India in the fourteenth and fifteenth centuries, usually in place of a signature. They became the object of scientific study and development in the late nineteenth century by a number of academics, notably Dr Henley Faulds, Francis Galton and Sir William Herschel.

Herschel was the first to use fingerprints in a formal and systematic way to identify criminals. Faulds was the first to propose that they be used to identify and eliminate suspects. The first fingerprint bureau was set up in Calcutta under Sir Edward Richard Henry, who is credited with the development of the classification system used in most English-speaking countries, although there is no doubt that much of the credit should also go to the two Indian fingerprint experts, Azizul Hacque and Hem Chandra Bose, who worked with him at the time. Scotland Yard set up the first fingerprint bureau in Britain in 1901, using the Henry classification system.

By the 1980s the fingerprint database had become unmanageable in terms of searching marks (prints found at the scene of a crime). The volume of material was such that manual systems could not cope. A mark would only be searched against the general database in very serious cases, where there seemed no other way are of taking the investigation forward. Those marks found at lower-level crime scenes such as burglaries were only searched against a force's target criminals or anyone that the investigator could put up as a suspect. At the time the service was confident that the identity of criminals was not a problem, but since automation a number of criminals have been found to have used more than one identity. In the early 1990s the process was computerized and the service got its first automatic fingerprint recognition (AFR) system. This meant that for the first time in decades the police were able to do what everyone thought they had always been able to do, i.e. check marks against the whole database. This development has played a significant part in improving police detection rates.

The Fingerprint

The palmar surfaces of the hand (and feet) are covered with ridges which are formed randomly in the foetus, developing unique patterns which do not change over a lifetime. No two fingerprints are the same, not even those of identical twins. The valleys between the ridges secrete on to all the surfaces with which they come into contact, leaving the ridge pattern. The secretions are a mixture of water, inorganic salts and organic material such as urea and amino acids. For a long time the prints on the surface at crime scenes, called latent prints or marks, could only be recovered in very limited circumstances, such as if they were recently deposited on a clean, nonporous surface. Now they can be recovered from most smooth surfaces using a variety of approaches ranging from the standard fingerprint powders, through reagents which can be fluoresced by an ultraviolet light and then photographed, to smoking superglue over the surface. It is normally necessary to remove the item or the part containing the fingerprint to a laboratory to do this.

The standard approach by most English forces is to use aluminium powder or flake, applying it with a fine bristle brush so as to minimize the danger of rubbing and thus damaging the print. This is adequate for most scenes of crime. The grey powder is visible against most other surfaces. Other colours are available if this is seen to be a problem. Ideally the SOCO wants the powder to adhere to the latent prints but not to the surface, so as to show a clear print. Aluminium flake is more sensitive (adherent) than powder but it may be too sensitive and, by clinging to the surface, cover (or paint) the latent (print) so as to obscure it. Which to use is a matter of professional judgement and SOCOs use their years of experience to decide where they are most likely to find prints and what techniques could and should be used to develop those that are there.

The only way to guarantee that the print is not disturbed is to ensure that it is examined *in situ*, only moving it as much as the examination itself requires. It is not safe to pick it up, no matter how it is done. Let us take a gun, for example. Picking it up with a handkerchief will ensure that you do not leave any prints on it, but it will almost certainly guarantee at the same time that any prints that are on it are at best smudged and damaged, and at worst completely rubbed off. The next favourite method on TV and film is to put a pen or pencil through the finger guard. This is great, unless of course there is a partial print on the trigger – not at all unlikely since that is where the finger is supposed to go. Finally, there is the pen put into the barrel. Again this is great as far as the outside of the weapon is concerned but if it was fired close enough to the victim the inside of the barrel may have minute traces of the victim's blood or clothing sticking to it, which would be invaluable in proving that it was the murder weapon; the pen will knock them off, so that they may not be recovered. The old rule for a crime scene of keeping your hands in your pockets at all times still holds good. Don't touch anything until the SOCO tells you he or she is finished with it.

Fingerprint Characteristics

The features of the fingerprint are called characteristics. They consist of three basic ridge patterns: the arch, the loop and the whorl. When these are present in a latent they give the fingerprint expert a good starter. The ridges themselves are made up of three basic minutiae: ridge endings, bifurcations and short ridges (or dots). These last are much shorter than the average ridge and are often contained by adjoining ridges, like a little island.

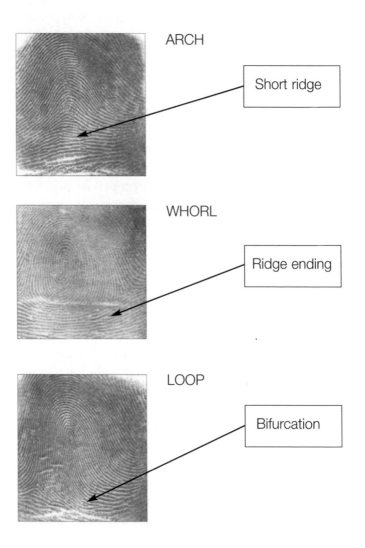

Figure 3: Fingerprint Characteristics

Matching Fingerprints

Until quite recently a fingerprint match could only be made if an expert could match sixteen characteristics in the mark found at the scene with the suspect's fingerprint. This was the highest number required by any agency worldwide; many were content with nine, and eleven was the standard in the USA. The UK has now moved to a qualitative rather than quantitative measure. This has been helped by the fact that there is now an approved certification of expert status in that the individual must have at least five years' experience and be qualified in the Professional Investigation Process. An expert can now make a positive identification based on fewer than sixteen characteristics if he or she can say that, taking the print as a whole, they are the same. This does introduce that element of interpretation already discussed which can undermine the objectivity of the evidence but it also allows for marginal identifications, for example with twelve characteristics, which would have previously been arbitrarily excluded regardless of the certainty of the expert that they were the same.

From a crime writer's point of view it should be borne in mind that the fewer characteristics the more the finding is a matter of opinion and not fact. This means that mistakes can be made. A very good recent example of this involved a DS in Scotland in 1997. DC McKie, a successful police officer in the Strathclyde Police, was involved in a murder inquiry in Kilmarnock. Her thumb print was allegedly found by the Scottish Crime Record Office (SCRO) experts in the kitchen of the murder house. She denied ever having been in the house. Since she was not involved in that element of the inquiry it would have been unprofessional of her to visit the scene at all, never mind being careless enough to leave a print. In the face of her denial she was arrested and charged with perjury. It took an enormous effort on her part and her supporters to have the Scottish Office acknowledge the error and agree to compensation. The case exemplifies the difficulty that can occur when expert evidence is taken as fact and not opinion.

Difficulties in Fingerprint Identification
The major difficulty is that the SOCO rarely gets a complete fingerprint at a scene. It is usually only a part of the print (called a partial) and it may contain the least useful elements in terms of identification. In addition, the expert has the following issues to deal with:

- since skin is flexible no two copies of the same finger-print will be exactly the same; there will always be some differences, no matter how slight
- it is not always easy to tell which finger the mark comes from, although its position on the object, the nature of the object itself, etc. will probably give some clues
- on partials the orientation may not be clear – which bits are the top, the bottom or the side. This is critical in working out the relative position of the characteristics
- the original police record against which the match is being made may not be a good one. The clarity of this print is critical. When they were taken using printer's ink on paper the quality was very variable and since the prisoner had inevitably been released before the prints reached the department it was difficult to get them redone. Today most, if not all, forces have Livescan, which allows an optical reader to capture the print so that its quality can be assessed immediately
- the suspect may have accumulated scars since the last time his or her fingerprints were taken. The scars will not be shown on the previous prints and they may cut through or distort key characteristics.

Taking Fingerprints

The police can take the fingerprints of anyone arrested for an offence. If the person is subsequently acquitted the prints must be destroyed, even if the suspect has a long record and the most recent set of prints is better than those currently on record. The law for retaining prints was set in more liberal times (despite the absence of the Human Rights Act), when Parliament believed that the privacy of the subject had some meaning.

When investigating offences police will often ask for 'elimination prints'. These are most often sought when it is necessary to eliminate all the people who had lawful access to the scene. They are also taken where there are a large number of possible suspects and a mark has been found at the scene. It is important to remember that the fact that the mark is not proven to be the suspect's does not eliminate him or her. Until the owner of the mark is identified it is impossible to know its worth or relevance and there may be other strong reasons for retaining the individual as a suspect. Elimination prints must be destroyed at the end of the inquiry and cannot be entered into the national database.

Taking fingerprints used to be a bit of a nightmare. A block had to be prepared, usually a long brass plate mounted on a wooden base. This was done by rolling out a thin layer of printer's ink. The prisoner then had each digit rolled in the ink and onto a fingerprint form. If the ink had been applied too liberally all you got was a black smudge; if the digit was rolled too lightly, or the subject had not been made to clean his or her hands first, part of the print would be missing or unreadable. Both thumbs were then taken simultaneously then a set of all four fingers of each hand. This was essential as the officer taking the prints may have put them on the form in the wrong order, or got the hands mixed up, something that happened surprisingly often.

Today fingerprints are all taken using optical readers and can be checked immediately against the national database to confirm identity, but the process is the same. The prints are also run against the force and national database of marks recovered from scenes of crime. Despite the difficulties, this makes a large number of hits. Since the whole process is now computerized it is now possible to take a laptop into the field loaded with a force's database so that checks can be done in the course of an operation with a suspect still present. If a secure encrypted link can be provided the laptop can be connected to the national database.

Fingerprints' Advantages

With the arrival of DNA, fingerprints have tended to slip into the background and their value has become less and less appreciated, with the spotlight being placed on their more glamorous competitor. However fingerprints are likely to continue as a mainstay of forensic detection for the following reasons:

- they have a track record of over 100 years in which no two fingerprints have ever been found to be identical and they are the basis for criminal identification in every police agency
- since every police agency uses them they are a worldwide tool and allow the certain exchange of information between agencies
- not only is there a vast existing database but it continues to expand daily
- in light of the current terrorist threat it is the only certain way of identifying suspects if their origins are in developing countries
- forensic practitioners continue to develop methods

for recovering prints where it was previously not possible – e.g. from materials damaged in a fire by the use of a play-dough-like material which removes the soot without damaging the print, or from metallic surfaces using a Kelvin probe

- it's cheap. In the UK every DNA analysis costs money whereas fingerprints have no additional costs
- even where the identity is not certain enough to support a conviction it can be very useful intelligence.

Genetic Fingerprinting

Dr Alex Jeffries of Leicester University was the first in the scientific community to notice that people's DNA has different patterns which can be used in identification. It was first used for forensic detection in 1987 to identify the rapist and murderer Colin Pitchfork. In 1983 a 15-year-old girl had been found raped and murdered on a lonely footpath outside the town of Narborough. Semen was recovered from the body but the killer was not identified and the case was left open. In 1986 another 15-year-old girl was found raped and murdered on another lonely footpath just outside the town. Both had been strangled and police believed that both were killed by the same man, partly due to the *modus operandi* and partly because semen samples found on both bodies came from a man with type A blood with an enzyme profile that was only shared by 10 per cent of the population. A 17-year-old youth, Richard Buckley, who had discovered the second body, was arrested for that killing. He confessed to the second murder but denied any involvement in the first.

Dr Jeffries offered to assist the investigating officer by testing the semen for its DNA profile. Everyone was surprised when it showed that both girls were raped by the same man but that that man wasn't Buckley. Five thousand local men were asked to give blood or saliva samples but no match was found. Later a man named Ian Kelly was heard bragging in a pub that he had stood in for his friend Colin Pitchfork. When Pitchfork was arrested and tested his sample was found to match the killer. DNA analysis very quickly became a major investigative tool.

DNA, deoxyribonucleic acid, is often described as the blueprint for the body's structure, but it is much more than that. A blueprint is essentially passive. It is read by somebody who then puts it into action. DNA not only has the pattern but it also issues instructions on how a cell will be built and when. It is a 1-foot-long strand in the form of a double helix. It fits into a cube one-millionth of an inch on each side and is present in nearly every body cell – not, strangely enough, in red blood cells, but only in white ones.

Every strand is made up of four bases, usually referred to by their initials of A, T, G and C, shorthand for their proper scientific names. Strings in DNA are described in terms of these letters, e.g. TTTGAAAACTTTAAATGATGA. Some DNA sequences encode information for the cell (coding DNA) and some don't appear to code anything that we know about at the present (non-coding or junk DNA). DNA is passed on through the sperm and egg cells, each containing about 3 billion bases that follow a well-defined sequence. The sequence of bases, coding and non-coding, varies from person to person and can be used to distinguish one person from another. The standard approach used by the FSS produces a result which enables their experts to state that the chances of getting two the same are one billion to one.

Reduced to its basics, DNA analysis is very straight-forward and now follows a thoroughly tested, reliable process. Every human's DNA, taken overall, is very similar. What makes it different is the pattern of bases in any given position on the DNA strand. If enough of these locations are tested it is possible to declare that their match is extremely unlikely to have happened by chance. The analysis is done as follows:

1. Targeted locations on the DNA are separated and amplified – caused to reproduce themselves.
2. The resulting fragments are separated and detected using electropherosis. The fragments have a slight negative charge and they are put into a gel which has a slight positive charge at one end. This causes the fragments to move towards the positive charge. The fragments are all of different lengths and the shorter ones move more quickly through the gel, causing the sample to stretch out in separated bands.
3. Fluorescent dyes which had been used in the targeting process then produce an image showing the bands clearly.
4. These bands are then compared with a standardized ladder and with the sample recovered from the crime scene.

The larger and fresher the sample the less danger there is of contamination and deterioration, thus more sequences can be tested, producing a more reliable result.

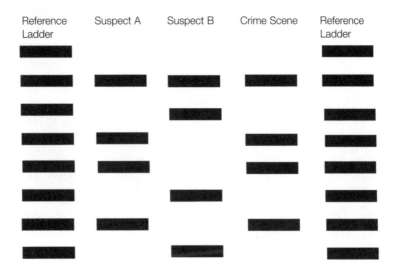

Figure 4: DNA Comparison Chart

Low Copy Number DNA Testing (LCN)
The initial approach to DNA analysis required quite large samples and took some time to produce results (2–4 weeks). A quicker and more sensitive process, which could work with small sample sizes, was soon developed. This is a combination of focusing the analysis on a limited number of locations on the DNA, technically called short tandem repeats (STR), and amplifying the sequence (causing them to reproduce themselves) through a process called polymerase chain reaction (PCR).

This approach can work on very small samples and can be carried out quite quickly – between forty-eight hours and a week depending on how much you are willing to pay. The method was further refined and developed so that minute samples of five to ten cells could be analysed successfully. Samples of this size can be obtained from a cup that has been drunk from or a pen used to write with.

From an investigator's viewpoint it looks too good to be true – and in some respects it is.

The process causes the sequence of DNA selected to reproduce over and over until there are enough copies to carry out an analysis. It is an exponential process. The original sequence is not copied again and again like a photostat, it produces copies and those copies are copied and so on. This has the advantage that a sample large enough for analysis is produced quite quickly but it also means that any rogue DNA is also copied and since it may have been present in the same strength as the targeted DNA it has the ability to produce false and thus misleading results.

Another problem is that in specimens that have been degraded, there is a possibility that some of the sequences that have been targeted will be missing, or that some of the bases will be missing from the targeted sequence. If this is so the resulting profile will only show a partial picture. To paraphrase Donald Rumsfeld, 'We don't know what we don't know', so there is always a danger that a completed profile will be different in some way from the original.

Both of these factors are important as they significantly affect the probability of error. The experts in this field give very large odds against the sequence occurring more than once, which appears to give the process a great deal of certainty. The problem is that the samples collected may not be truly random. For example if the murder occurs in a small, remote village, many of the inhabitants may be related, two brothers will have very similar profiles and cousins may also have a higher than average similarity of profile. This means that it is necessary not only to calculate the odds of a sample randomly reappearing but to calculate the odds of one reappearing in the context of the investigation.

Where the crime scene is undisturbed the SOCOs can be

reasonably certain that the minute samples they recover are uncontaminated by any subsequent contact. They cannot tell whether the same cup was drunk from by two people or whether two people used the same pen (unless it was a man and woman, when the sex chromosome may be present and may assist). Practices have been developed for recovering samples so that they will be safely transferred from the scene to the laboratory. At the laboratory there are a number of processes to ensure that any contamination is identified and, according to the CPS, 'the statistical interpretation of the results allows for the possibility that some of the DNA may be due to contamination or other effects caused by working with such low-level samples'.

All this means that the profiles produced by LCN from specimens currently recovered from crime scenes are probably reliable. The same cannot be said for those recovered in the past where cross contamination was not a consideration when they were being recovered or handled. In these cases the safest way to approach low copy number analysis is to see it as being persuasive rather than conclusive evidence, i.e. safer and of more weight if there is other evidence to corroborate it.

I have tried to discuss this issue in a non-technical way. If you want to take it any further I recommend the following websites:

Wikipedia
http://www.wikipedia.org/wiki/Genetic_finger-printing
The language in this entry is quite technical but it does provide access to outside links and is an easy way of keeping up to date. It also describes the difficulties in statistical interpretation that can produce the prosecutor's and the defender's fallacies.

Scientific Testimony
http://www.scientific.org/tutorials/articles/riley/riley.htm
This a scientific description of the process for non-scientists
which worked for me.

PBS (Public Broadcasting Service – USA)
http://www.pbs.org/wgbh/nova/sheppard/lab01.html
This is aimed at older children but the 'hands on' feel of the
virtual lab helped me understand how the process worked.

CHAPTER 4

Profiling and Serial Killers

Despite what you are about to read I am a great fan of Cracker and Val McDermid's Dr Tony Hill. However profiling in real life is a pale shadow of its fictional counterpart. The theory of profiling was first developed in Britain by Dr David Canter, who built on the approach of the FBI's Behavioral Analysis Unit. That unit was staffed by investigators rather than psychologists and, according to Dr Canter, used a pragmatic rather than academic approach to profiling, relying on their intuitive interpretation of every case based on their experience rather than developing a set of principles that could be applied to any case.

The attraction of profiling is that it gives the investigator a picture of the criminal thus enabling the search for a suspect to be limited in some way – e.g. where he or she lives and works, any criminal history, or whether he or she is married or single. The difficulty is that, for a number of reasons, it is not at all reliable and its use can bring with it significant dangers.

Profiling Principles

I found it difficult to discern clear principles from Dr Canter's work and he appears now to be focusing more on the issue of geographic (where the suspect is likely to live or work) rather than psychological profiling. The few that I can find from the literature appear to be as follows.

Commuter/Marauder
This principle is more successful when considering a series of rapes/murders which occur in clusters in bigger towns and cities, as it lies in developing a relationship between the location of the crimes and where the criminal lives (or sometimes works). Commuters live outside the area of the crimes and focus their offending in one or two specific areas where they feel comfortable, perhaps because they have lived or worked there at some time, or believe that it is where they are more likely to find the type of victim they seek. Marauders live in the area where the offences occur. The problem for the detective is that until he or she catches the criminal, it is unclear whether they are a commuter or a marauder, as this factor is not predictably associated with any other, for example if the marauder always attacked their victim in a public area it would be possible to associate these two factors. All the investigator has are clusters of similar crimes probably committed by the same person who feels comfortable working in that area – and he or she knows that already.

Three Types of Rapist/Murderer
Dr Canter describes three different types of rapists according to how they treat the victim: as an object, as a victim or as a person. He believes that this can be useful as each has distinctive features which may assist the investigator to identify potential suspects.

The victim as an object. Here the rapist is only interested in the victim as something to control. He has no feelings towards them, not even anger, and only uses them to fulfil his inner fantasies. Features of this type of offender are:

- the assault is made in public and the victim is usually a target of opportunity
- he will tend to attack the same type of person – young girls, older women, gay men
- the control may continue after death – necrophilia, retention of the body or body parts, cannibalism
- he is unlikely to be living with a partner.

The victim as vehicle. This person has much in common with the first. The key difference is that he sees the role that empathy can play although he has never or rarely felt it for anyone, certainly not his victim. She is seen as someone to be exploited so that the killer can somehow restore himself to being the person in control. Features of this type are:

- he may have a history of unsuccessful relationships
- the initial contact may not be threatening to the victim
- the location may carry some meaning for the attacker
- emotional events in the killer's life may provide the trigger for the assaults to begin or temporarily stop
- he will tend to be a commuter
- he will be from the older end of the attacker age range, i.e. late twenties or early thirties.

The victim as a person. This attacker come as close to 'normal' as is possible in that he tries to empathize with the victim and succeeds in his own distorted way. During the course of the assault he will attempt to develop a relationship with the victim, perhaps by asking about boyfriends and other personal details. In this way he confuses the rape with a real sexual relationship. Features of this type are:

- he moves to rape from other crime, especially burglary
- he may stalk the victim first
- he may break into the victim's house and wait for her to return
- he may be living with a partner although it is probable that the relationship will be a difficult or uneasy one in which he continually seeks to dominate.

Other Descriptive Factors
The literature describes the following factors as being common to serial killers. It does not give any clues about how many of the seven factors you are likely to find, or the likelihood of any particular one being present. Serial killers tend to:

- be working-class, in unskilled jobs providing a low income and little job satisfaction
- come from families that were dysfunctional in serious ways – rejection by one or both parents is a feature
- be poor at forming relationships
- be the runts of the family, small in stature
- have been poor achievers at school
- have become involved in minor crime at an early age
- have 'psychopathic' personalities (whatever that may mean – my psychopath may be your sane but obsessed collector).

Unfortunately most of these factors apply to most of the criminals I have come across so their use as a reliable predictor is questionable, and any study of serial killers will provide examples to which none, other than sexual fantasies and psychopathic personalities, apply – look at Dennis Nilsen and Ted Bundy. This list look impressive at first sight but from an investigator's point of view the more factors there are the less useful they become as some or most of them could apply to anyone. In *Wire in the Blood* Val McDermid lists thirty factors, then adds 'a psychopathic personality'. Anyone satisfying most of the factors would need to be either locked up or a saint.

Problems with Profiling

From a police perspective I have two major concerns about profiling. First, the methodology demands that it can only be based on criminals who have been caught; secondly, it can tempt the SIO and his or her team to become too narrowly focused too quickly, and keeping an open mind is a key skill for an SIO.

Only the Ones We've Caught

Profiling is based on the analysis of crimes and people who have been arrested for them. This means that the profile is based on the least successful or most unlucky criminals. It is not surprising, therefore, to find that they were poor achievers at school. Dr Harold Shipman, intelligent, with a stable family background, the father of three sons and apparently a good husband and father, is reckoned to have killed around 250 people, mostly older women. There is some evidence that he began killing people in the early 1970s and he was not arrested until 1998. Even his arrest was triggered by the fact that he had forged a will for his latest victim, and some interpret this as a desire on his part to be caught. While it is probable that his case is an unusual one and his position gave him fairly unique access to potential victims, the fact that he got away with his crimes for so long and does not fit any of the factors described in the profile powerfully shows that there could be an unknown number of Shipmans out there, knowledge about whom would fundamentally change the principles upon which profiling is based.

Keeping an Open Mind

Closing down the options too quickly is the greatest danger that profiling presents. As I have said, the SIO must keep an open mind, especially at the beginning of an investigation or when it has run into the buffers. The dangers of failing to do so are only too clear, as the cases of Colin Stagg and the Yorkshire Ripper show.

In 1992 Rachel Nickell was found brutally murdered on Wimbledon Common with her young son clutching her bloodied body. The case created a predictable public outrage and the pressure on the inquiry team to get a result must have been immense. Colin Stagg came into the frame as he was seen frequently on the common and he fitted the profile developed by Paul Britton, a criminal psychologist used by the SIO. As a result Mr Stagg was made the target of a 'honey pot' operation and was induced into making a number of compromising statements, none of which amounted to an admission. After spending fourteen months in prison and having his life destroyed by the way the murder and the trial were reported he was acquitted. Another man, Robert Napper, has since been charged with the murder and was due to face trial in November 2008.

The Yorkshire Ripper case shows how focusing on one line of inquiry to the exclusion of all others can cripple it. The murder team there received tape recordings and letters from a man claiming to be The Ripper. The voice on the tapes had a Geordie accent and the SIO, Detective Chief Superintendent George Oldfield, decided to focus the inquiry on this lead. A detective who interviewed Sutcliffe during this time put him into the 'strong suspect' category but was overruled as Sutcliffe did not have a Geordie accent.

The most infamous case in British police history showing the danger of having a closed mind was the mass murder of the Bamber family in Essex in 1985. Jeremy Bamber and his sister Sheila had both been adopted by Ralph and June Bamber. Sheila married and had young twin sons. On the break-up of her marriage she became depressed and was diagnosed as paranoid schizophrenic. At the time of the killings it is known that she had stopped taking her medication and there were concerns for the twins' well-being. At 3.26 on the morning of the 7th of August Jeremy Bamber telephoned the local police to tell them that his father had just telephoned him saying, 'Sheila's got the gun, she's gone crazy, come over here quickly.' The call had then been ended and when he phoned back he could only get an engaged tone. He told the police that his sister had a history of mental illness and he arranged to meet them at his parents' house at White House Farm.

Bamber arrived at the farmhouse shortly after the first police and by 5.30 they were joined by armed police. They discussed Sheila's history with Bamber and eventually, at 7.30, broke into the farmhouse. They found Ralph Bamber's body in the kitchen, which was in disarray and looked as if a struggle had taken place; June Bamber's body was in the main bedroom; the twins were found shot in the head, lying in their beds, and Sheila's body lay by the side of her parents' bed. They had all been shot with the .22 rifle that Sheila was found clutching to her chest. She had two gunshot wounds to the throat. The rifle was bolt action, which meant that the bolt had to be worked between shots to eject the used round, reload the chamber and cock the trigger. The SIO immediately took the view that he was dealing with a mass murder of the family by Sheila, after which she took her own life.

The police not only allowed Bamber to have the house cleaned very soon after the killing but actually assisted him in the process, thus removing almost all the evidence and compromising what was left.

Following the inquest Jeremy Bamber's behaviour began to raise the suspicions of both the police and Ralph and June's relatives. When one of them, David Boutflour, was clearing some items from the farmhouse he found the .22's noise moderator (silencer) in the farmhouse gun cupboard. He saw that it had red paint marks which looked as if they had come from some paint damage in the kitchen and that there was a grey hair stuck to the end. He brought this to the attention of the police and they had the silencer examined forensically. That examination found that the paint was the same as that in the kitchen and was consistent with damage seen there, and that there were spots of blood inside the silencer which were the same blood type as Sheila's (DNA was not used at that time). With the silencer mounted it would have been impossible for Sheila to shoot herself and she could not have shot herself then removed the silencer to put it back in the gun cupboard. A body of circumstantial evidence was then developed pointing to Jeremy Bamber as the killer which included the following facts:

- he appeared to have telephoned his girlfriend telling her about the murder before his phone call to the police
- he was in debt
- his girlfriend at the time of the killings said that he had talked of murdering his parents.

He was arrested, tried and convicted. He has appealed three times unsuccessfully, and still protests his innocence. I have not seen enough of the original evidence to make a judgement, and most of the accounts of the murder are given from a partial viewpoint. But the key issue for me is the fact that the SIO's decision that Sheila had killed the others, then committed suicide, was made without enough consideration of the evidence available. Given the scale of the killings it is certain that there would have been enough forensic evidence at the scene, Jeremy Bamber's house and on the route between the two locations to provide definite proof either way. The fact that the house was cleaned and that evidence was not collected until several weeks later effectively deprived the investigators of the bulk of the forensic, and thus objective, evidence, leaving them to rely on circumstantial, therefore interpretative, evidence.

Dr Canter does not appear to appreciate this danger. In his book *Criminal Shadows* he describes how the FBI agent Roy Hazelwood of the Behavioral Science Unit 'knew' on entering a crime scene that 'a black assailant who lived in the vicinity had done it'. If I were an SIO and a profiler said this to me I'd kick him off the team immediately because of the danger that he would then build a profile where the factors that supported his 'knowledge' would be recognized and maybe even enhanced, and those that didn't would be ignored.

This certainty still appears to be part of Dr Canter's approach. In an article in the *Guardian* (27 December 2007) he discussed the Jill Dando shooting and said that had he been consulted he could have told the investigators that over 80 per cent of killers who escaped on foot live within 525 yards of the crime. It took police over a year to question and arrest Barry George, a man with a record of stalking celebrities. He lived within the 525-yard radius. He went on to say, 'The point is not that it was Barry George and that I turned out to be right. The point is that, with a focused investigation, the police could have got to him a great deal earlier than they did and eliminated him if necessary.'

In fact Barry George had been treated as a suspect for some time, but a profiling approach based on more than distance would appear to exclude him. He is a fantasist, adopting a number of pseudonyms including Paul Gadd (Gary Glitter) and Barry Bulsara (Freddie Mercury). He is described as inept and disorganized and has suffered from learning difficulties all his life. Jill Dando's killer on the other hand was either very organized or incredibly lucky. He shot her at her front door in the middle of the day in a central London street. The front gardens in this part of London are tiny, only a few steps separating the garden gate from the front door. The killer forced Miss Dando to the ground and effectively used her head as a silencer. Only two people saw him walk away and their descriptions do not appear to readily fit Barry George. The streets in this part of London are narrow, with cars parked on both sides. The danger of being blocked in by a double-parked car is ever present so the safest exit from the scene would be on a motorcycle or on foot to a rendezvous point to be picked up. On 15 November 2007 the Appeal Court found the conviction of Barry George to be unsafe and ordered a retrial. He was acquitted on 1 August 2008.

Catching Serial Killers

If profiling is of such limited use, how are serial killers caught? Usually it is a mixture of arrogance and bad luck on their part and solid police work. Their arrogance shows in trying one more time, even when they know the police have mounted a large operation to find them; bad luck occurs in that a member of the public or a police officer sees something suspicious and solid policing makes sure that this break is exploited. To see how these factors work together we will look at some of the more notorious British serial killers:

- Dennis Nilsen and Peter Sutcliffe because of the number of people they killed before being caught
- Robert Black to look at the limitations of geographic profiling
- since their case involved the first use of profiling, the 'railway murderers' John Duffy and David Mulcahy.

Dennis Nilsen
Between 1979 and 1987 Dennis Nilsen killed sixteen men, and five others survived his attacks. His *modus operandi* was to pick up men in gay bars and clubs and take them back to his flat. He usually selected men who were homeless or whose absence would not be noticed. He was discovered only because he overloaded his drains with bits of body. A drain-clearance operator was called to the blocked sewer outside Nilsen's home. In the inspection chamber he found what he thought were bits of human flesh. He reported this to his supervisor who advised him to 'sleep on it' and call the police in the morning if he was still worried about it. This he duly did and DCI Peter Jay went with him to inspect the drain. In the meantime Nilsen had been told about his visit and had done his best to ensure that the sewer was clear by the time the police arrived.

However DCI Jay still found some bones that he thought were knuckle bones. He took them to Professor Bower of Charing Cross Hospital, a highly experienced Home Office pathologist. He identified the bones as being neck bones and recognized marks on them as being consistent with

ligature marks, indicating that the person had been strangled. So the police had two pieces of luck: the discovery of
body parts, and the fact that they were examined by a
highly experienced pathologist, as not every pathologist
may have recognized the significance of the marks.

DCI Jay returned to Nilsen's flat where there took place
one of the shortest and easiest interrogations of a murder
suspect in history.

DCI Jay: Mr Nilsen, your drains were blocked with
           human remains.
Nilsen: How awful.
DCI Jay: Now don't mess me about, where is the rest
           of the body?
Nilsen: They're in two plastic bags in the other room.
           I'll show you.
DCI Jay: I thought so. What's been going on here?
Nilsen: It's a long story. I'll tell you everything.

In fact there were the parts of two bodies in the bedroom
and two heads in the fridge.

Profiling would not have helped with Nilsen. He killed
all his victims in his flat and disposed of the remains
through the drains. There could be no geographic pattern
to follow. His motivation did not appear to be sexual as
consensual sex had already taken place and at least ten
men passed through his flat for every one who was
attacked. Even if there had been a pattern of deaths it is not
clear that Nilsen would have fitted any profile. He was
described as a 'grey man'. He was reasonably well
educated and at the time of the killings had a responsible
job in the Manpower Services Commission. He had no
difficulty in finding worthwhile employment, he had been
a probationary police officer and had trained as a chef.

The Yorkshire Ripper

Peter Sutcliffe attacked twenty-one women between 1975 and 1981, killing thirteen of them. Most were prostitutes. Most were killed using a hammer blow to the head followed by knife slashing to the stomach and groin area. The distinctive *m.o.* and selection of victims made it clear to investigators that they were looking for one killer from a very early stage. The inquiry was complicated by the fact that the attacks occurred in three police force areas and the police had not yet developed protocols for dealing with this nor a computer system to support it. The spread of the attacks in both time and geography made it impossible for police to mount an effective patrol strategy and at that time there was not the CCTV coverage which was critical to the success of the recent Suffolk case where Steve Wright killed five women over a three-week period.

On 2 January 1981 Sutcliffe was stopped by police driving a car with false number plates. He was accompanied by a prostitute. He was arrested and at the police station was questioned at length because of his similarity to the description of the Ripper. The arresting officer, a Sergeant Ring, decided to go back and search the place where he had arrested Sutcliffe as the latter had asked to be allowed to go behind an oil storage tank to urinate. There he found a hammer, a knife and a rope. After two days of questioning Sutcliffe suddenly broke and admitted that he was the Ripper. His confession took over sixteen hours and filled thirty-four pages. Some weeks later he claimed that a voice from God had told him to attack women.

In theory profiling should have worked in the Ripper case, had it been available. Sutcliffe not only had a very consistent *m.o.* – only five of the murdered woman were not prostitutes, all bar one was attacked outside, and a ball-pein hammer and knife were used in most of the assaults. He had also developed the 'signature' in that he mutilated the victim by slashing the stomach and groin areas, even when they were already dead. Yet if he is examined against a list of profiling characteristics the likelihood of a profile helping to identify him looks poor:

- although working-class he used redundancy money from one job to become qualified as an HGV driver and had a fairly good employment record
- he was described as a quiet, shy boy
- his family were dysfunctional in that the father was a bully and the mother a doormat. Both had fairly public affairs. This does fit the profile but is not the sort of information that is available to detectives who are trying to prioritize a list of thousands
- he had met his wife in 1967, married her in 1974 and their marriage had lasted through a series of miscarriages
- he is of average height
- he left school at fifteen but that was normal for working-class boys of that age at that time and this needs to be seen in the light of his HGV qualification
- he had no previous criminal record.

If profiling had been used it is likely that Sutcliffe would have been closer to the bottom than the top of any list. His stable employment background, apparently settled marriage and lack of criminal record would probably have been enough to ensure that he never made a 'strong suspect' list because he didn't fit the profile, just as had the fact that he did not have a Geordie accent.

Although the inquiry itself could never be considered a

success it is worth considering the effort that the three forces put into the inquiry:

- 260,000 people interviewed
- 32,000 statements taken
- 5.4 million car registration numbers checked
- 40 tonnes of paperwork accumulated
- 250 detectives engaged in the inquiry over three years.

Sutcliffe was interviewed nine times and as we have seen one detective at least thought that he should be treated as a 'strong suspect'. At the time of his arrest a line of inquiry was being pursued which might have identified him. A new five-pound note was found in the discarded handbag of one of the victims, Jean Jordan. It had been traced back to a wages payment which produced a list of 300 employees. The sequence of notes containing the five-pound note would have reduced that list to thirty and Sutcliffe was in this group.

Robert Black

I have included Black as his case shows the difficulties created when a killer is mobile and moves across not just police areas like Sutcliffe, but even jurisdictions (this is a more common problem in the USA – the issues this raises are discovered in Chapter 6).

On 30 July 1982 Susan Maxwell, aged eleven, was abducted from Cornhill on Tweed, just on the English side of the English/Scottish border. Her body was found dumped by the side of the road near Uttoxeter, Staffordshire.

On 8 July 1983 Caroline Hogg, aged five, was abducted from Portobello just outside Edinburgh. Her naked body was found in a ditch in Leicestershire. Decomposition of both bodies made it impossible to determine the exact cause of death, or whether they had been raped.

On 26 March 1986 Sarah Harper, aged ten, was abducted from Leeds. Her naked and strangled body was found dumped in the River Trent near Nottingham a month later.

All three bodies were found within thirty miles of one another and the common *m.o.* led to the inquiries being linked. By the time of Sarah Harper's murder the HOLMES system had been developed and the inquiry had computer support. The pattern of the killings and bodies indicated that the killer probably travelled as part of his occupation – perhaps as a salesman or a lorry driver. An enormous police investigation was launched and every lead was followed up; for example in Sarah Maxwell's case a maroon Triumph 2000 was suspect and 19,000 drivers were seen, interviewed and eliminated; similarly in Caroline Hogg's case a blue Cortina was suspect and this led to 20,000 drivers being seen, interviewed and eliminated.

On 14 July 1990 near Stow in Scotland, about thirty miles from the border with England, Mandy Wilson, aged six, was seen by a member of the public being bundled into the back of a van. He called police and was able to give them a registration number. Miraculously the van passed the witness when he was still talking to the police and it was successfully stopped and Black was arrested. One of the officers at the scene of the arrest was Mandy's father. She was found bound and gagged, stuffed into a sleeping bag in the back of the van. Had Black not been stopped she would probably have suffocated in a relatively short time.

Black pleaded guilty to the abduction of Mandy Wilson but has never admitted abducting and killing the other three. He was tried and found guilty of their murder in May 1994. He was sentenced to life imprisonment and the judge recommended that he serve at least thirty-five years, making him eighty-two before he would be released.

Unlike Sutcliffe, Black fitted almost all the academic criteria.

- he was working-class, a poor time-keeper and lucky to find and keep a job where he could work unsupervised
- there is evidence that he suffered physical abuse at the first home where he was fostered and that he was sexually abused in one of the children's homes where he lived
- although he appeared sociable, was a regular player on the amateur darts circuit and liked football, he never formed any friendships and had few girlfriends
- he was clever enough to get in to a grammar school but made nothing of it
- his record of indecent assaults from an early age (twelve) showed that he regularly indulged in sexual fantasies
- he was convicted of a serious sexual assault at the age of seventeen although it was recorded as a relatively minor one. Paedophile killers are more likely to have a criminal record and some of their convictions may be for sex offences, although they may not be particularly serious – simply being a peeping Tom.

Would profiling have helped to find Black sooner? Geographic profiling certainly would not. The range of locations would have defeated any attempts to focus enquiries. Black lived in and worked from London while the girls were abducted from the north and their bodies were dumped in the Midlands. Any such focus would only have misled the inquiry.

A psychological profile, however, might have helped to

identify him. After his conviction the SIO was criticized for restricting the possible suspects to people with a criminal record for more serious offences. This meant that Black was never in the system. The SIO justified this on the understandable grounds that the inquiry could not have handled the bigger list a wider net would have created. The effort required to eliminate suspects cannot be underestimated, as all the facts that they give need to be corroborated before they can be eliminated. A profile might have enabled the inquiry to broaden the net to include minor sex offences as it could then have been used as a filter to prioritize these 'possibles'. This is easy to say with the benefit of hindsight knowing that Black did it. I am not sure that any SIO today would be willing to put the level of faith in the profile that such an approach would demand.

The Railway Murders
Finally we come to the case that introduced the use of profiling in Britain. Between 1982 and 1985 John Duffy and David Mulcahy abducted nineteen women from or near railway stations in north London and raped them. Duffy matched the description given by some victims and he was put on an identificiation (ID) parade but was not identified. Mulcahy was only routinely questioned and released.

On 29 December 1985 Alison Day was abducted at Hackney railway station, repeatedly raped her and then strangled with a piece of string.

On 17 April 1986 Maartje Tamboezer, aged fifteen, was attacked near West Horsley railway station in Surrey. She was raped, strangled with string and an attempt was made to set her body on fire.

On 18 May 1986 Anne Locke was abducted from the Brookmans Park railway station in Hertfordshire then raped and murdered.

93

The Metropolitan Police (Met) had already linked the murder of Alison Day with the previous rapes and the SIO of the inquiry recognized similarities with the murder of Maartje Tamboezer. Both murders were linked and the joint inquiry was now led by Detective Chief Superintendent Vince McFadden of Surrey. Dr Canter, then of Surrey University, had already been contacted by the Met to discuss the possibility of developing a profile. This process was continued by Vince McFadden, who gave Dr Canter a couple of detectives to assist him in order to speed up the work. The profile that Dr Canter developed fitted Duffy in thirteen of the seventeen characteristics.

Duffy was in the list of over 2,000 'possibles', and had been close enough to the description given by one of the victims to have been put in an ID parade. It was also known that he had raped his wife, from whom he was separated, at knifepoint and she had complained that he had forced her to have sex while they were together by tying her up. After he became known to the inquiry his behaviour took a bizarre turn; he appeared battered and bruised at a police station claiming to have been attacked and as a result having lost his memory. He was admitted to a psychiatric hospital for treatment for this 'amnesia'. Later an associate of Duffy's came forward to say that he had beaten Duffy up at his request so that Duffy could convince the police that he had amnesia.

Duffy was then targeted and put under surveillance. He was arrested in the act of stalking a woman in a park. A search of his house revealed the same unusual string that had been used to bind the murder victims. Forensic evidence of fibres on his clothing, blood-typing and a positive identification on an ID parade built up a very strong case against him. He was found guilty of two of the three murders and five rapes and was given life imprisonment with a recommendation that he serve at least thirty years. He did not admit to any of the offences, so did not give any information about his accomplice, Mulcahy.

In 1997, while in prison, Duffy admitted the murders and his role in the murder of Anne Locke to a counsellor. He also implicated Mulcahy, who had been a friend since childhood, claiming that Mulcahy was the instigator and major planner of the killings. The cases were reopened and DNA recovered which corroborated Duffy's accusations. Mulcahy was arrested in 1999 and found guilty of the murder and rape of the three women and of seven more rapes. He was given three life sentences for the murders and twenty-four years for the rapes.

At first sight the fact that Duffy hit Dr Canter's profile in thirteen of the seventeen characteristics looks impressive, and it was treated as such at the time. A closer analysis in the light of Duffy's admissions and Mulcahy's convictions, however, significantly changes its impact. Despite the fact that the police were certain that there were two assailants in most of the rapes and were pretty sure that Duffy had an accomplice in the murders, no profile was developed for a possible second assailant.

Although there was a high probability that two were involved no allowance appeared to be made for the fact that the profile could have been a composite of two men. In *Criminal Shadows*, Dr Canter describes his reasoning to support the profile: 'He [the killer] had become a lone attacker.' But Duffy was raping with Mulcahy in July 1985, and Alison Day's murder was in December of that year. The pattern did not indicate that either rapist had begun to work alone and police had always suspected there was a second killer.

Dr Canter continued: 'It would be strange indeed that a man could keep a deep, caring relationship with his wife and still go out frequently with a friend or on his own to rape and then murder.' But Mulcahy was married and stayed married until his arrest in 1999.

Dr Canter says: 'The viciousness of Duffy's assault on the 15-year-old Maartje Tamboezer seemed to me very difficult to associate with the actions of a man who had been involved in bringing up children himself.' Mulcahy has four children.

You can see from all that I have written that I am sceptical about the usefulness of profiling. I have found no cases in the UK where it has played a significant role in the investigation. Even in the USA where there is a greater need and the technique has a longer history it would not have helped to identify that country's most ruthless serial killer, Ted Bundy, as he did not come anywhere near fitting the classic background – he was a graduate, was involved in politics and changed his *m.o.* at least three times, whereas his treatment of victims as an object would, in profiling terms, suggest a poor achiever making disorganized attacks.

So can a crime writer use profiling? It is a question of fact and degree as the lawyers say. Cracker was phenomenally popular, as is Val McDermid's Dr Tony Hill. If the characters are believable, the plot is good and the text persuasive it can obviously be a useful crime-writing device. But remember that in *Wire in the Blood* the killer was initially identified by a straightforward analysis of missing persons reports together with a trawl of local newspapers to see what they coincided with. The psychological element came later – quite like real life actually.

CHAPTER 5

Other Serious Crimes

So far I have generally focused on murder, as it is the crime most commonly used by crime writers as a focus for the plot. Now I would like to look at four other crimes which are powerful enough to be a focus for the main plot or are often ancillary to it and which, if serious enough, get the same police response as murder – the appointment of an SIO, the setting up of an incident room etc.

Rape

Serial killers often start out as serial rapists and rape is the sort of 'serial' offence in which *m.o.*, signature, profiling and forensic evidence figure heavily. Before the Sexual Offences Act 2003 the law on rape and other non-consensual sex was a mess for a number of reasons. First, there were essentially only two sex offences: rape – the penetration of the vagina by a penis without consent; and indecent assault – touching, stroking etc. which was considered indecent or which was carried out in a sexual context. The old law failed in two important aspects: penetration and consent.

Penetration

The law has now been amended to catch up with the many and different forms of perverse attacks suffered by victims today so that it now covers penetration of the vagina, mouth or anus by just about anything if it is done for sexual gratification and without consent.

Consent

In *R. v. Morgan* [1976] AC 182, the House of Lords ruled that the prosecution, and thus the victim, had to prove not just that intercourse had taken place without consent but that the defendant was either reckless or did not care whether or not she consented. An honest belief of consent on his part, even if it was not reasonable, was enough to evade liability. The Act now makes it clear that the victim only has to prove penetration and lack of consent; the defendant must show that his belief that she consented was 'reasonable . . . having regard to all the circumstances'.

Vulnerable persons

The Act also consolidated and improved the degree of protection afforded to vulnerable people such as children and those with learning difficulties. It effectively means that doing anything indecent to them, getting them to do anything indecent or getting them to view anything indecent is an absolute offence – consent is not an issue.

Difficulties

Despite all these changes the conviction rate for rape is still abysmally low – only 6 per cent. This low figure must be seen in the context that only 20 per cent of rape is reported at all. The British crime survey found that only 8 per cent of rapes were committed by strangers, and that the greatest danger comes from a partner or ex-partner. This group commit 45 per cent of rapes. It is in this light that the poor conviction rate must be seen. Since intercourse is usually admitted, the critical issue for the jury is whether or not the woman consented. Crucial to this is her credibility versus his.

It must be remembered that the jury knows nothing of the circumstances of the crime or the characters of the victim and the alleged rapist, other than what they learn from the trial process. If the victim appears cold and in control, or hysterical, or evasive, or uncertain of the facts then this is the only picture that they have of her. This presents difficulties for a rape victim for a number of reasons:

- rape is a traumatic event and the victim may still be suffering from post-traumatic stress disorder, which may affect her behaviour, especially under hostile cross-examination
- she may not have a clear memory of the event or may be too embarrassed to mention vital details either to the investigator or in the public arena of the courtroom
- the rapist may have used a date rape drug such as Rohypnol or GHB (Gamma-Hydroxybutyric Acid). Her difficulties are compounded in this case by the fact that there is usually a delay in reporting this type of rape and it is difficult to detect both of these drugs after any period of time (twenty-four hours in the case of GHB and seventy-two with Rohypnol). I hate the expression 'date rape' as it somehow diminishes the victim, but like 'joy-riding' it is now part of the language
- in date rape the victims may exaggerate the degree of force used or threatened, or lie about the amount of alcohol/drugs they had taken in order to

maximize their chances of being taken seriously by the police

- in stranger rape victims often exaggerate the rapist's size and describe him as better looking than he is in real life (although they always seem, in my experience, to get the eyes right).

All these factors make the rape victim an easy target in cross-examination and since the key issue is her credibility they are the factors the defence will focus on.

The final difficulty that the victim faces in court is that she will often only be able to deal with the experience by detaching herself from it. This may make her appear unaffected by the rape to the jury and may affect their interpretation of the event. The difficulty is compounded by the stupid legal convention that the prosecuting barrister will only see her for the first time in court and will have used the written statement in assessing her potential as a witness. He or she will not be aware of any difficulties that the investigator faced in getting the women to describe the event and the rapist. This convention is now, finally, under review.

Paedophile Crime

The Sexual Offences Act 2003 also comprehensively expanded the law in relation to sexual offences with children to ensure that any sexual act involving or in the presence or view of a child is an offence. It also created the offences of grooming and inciting a child to engage in any sexual activity.

The Offender

Sexual attacks by strangers on children are still relatively rare events. It is a difficult and dangerous crime to carry out and if the attacker allows the child to live they know that there will be both a witness and forensic evidence to help convict them. Paedophiles prefer to groom both the child and family, getting themselves into a position of trust by convincing the parents that they can be relied on to look after the child, then ensuring the child's silence through threats or promises of rewards. They are without doubt the most difficult people to deal with in policing terms as they are devious, persistent and, until discovery, have usually persuaded both the family and the local community that they are well-intentioned and trustworthy.

The Victim

In law a child is anyone up to the age of eighteen. I could write a whole chapter dedicated to the ages selected by statute in determining whether a child can or cannot do something and the degree of protection that they do or do not deserve which could provide its own social commentary reflecting the attitudes of the time the law was enacted. As far as being a victim of crime is concerned the key ages are thirteen and sixteen. Anyone having sex with a child under the age of thirteen commits rape, as it is impossible for him or her to give her consent. Sixteen is the age of consent for sex for both boys and girls but if a male under the age of twenty-four has sex with a girl under sixteen he may not be prosecuted if he can show that he reasonably believed that she was sixteen or over.

Apart from consent, age is a key issue in terms of the victim's credibility and usefulness as a witness. After the age of twelve children are probably as good a witness as they will ever be as adults, whereas children under the

101

age of six rarely make good witnesses for a number of reasons:

- they don't have the language to explain what happened, especially grooming and threats or promises
- they are not robust enough to withstand even gentle examination never mind cross-examination
- their memory or ability to recall incidents in any logical order is often poor.

The key factor is the child's intelligence and emotional development.

Much has been done to protect child witnesses from the effects of the defendant's presence in court. Evidence can now be given behind a screen or via a CCTV link; the judge may decide that everyone should take off their wigs and gowns to make the atmosphere less formal and intimidating and, best of all, the judge can rule that the defendant cannot cross-examine the child personally but only through a lawyer (this can also be done with rape victims).

Forces now have specific departments to deal with 'family' crime, such as domestic violence and child abuse in all its forms. The child victim will always be interviewed by a specialist officer who has had extensive training and he or she will be supported by a specialist social worker. The parents will not be allowed to be present as their emotional reactions cannot be relied on and it is essential that the investigator gets the child's version of what happened as best the child can remember and articulate that memory. Anatomically correct dolls help greatly in this with younger children. There are proposals that TV footage of interviews become the sole evidence of children, but this subverts the ability of defendants to test the evidence against them – a main pillar of our confrontational legal system.

When a child is being abused the non-abusive partner either:

- knows that it is going on but ignores it in order to keep the abusing partner happy
- knows it is going on but is in denial, as to acknowledge it would require a confrontation with the abusing partner
- genuinely has not noticed what is going on.

In any case the exposure of the abuse causes the family and its network of friends and acquaintances to implode, with the blame being placed squarely on the non-abusing partner, regardless of culpability, by both herself and the community. This is one of the many difficulties that the Family Liaison Officer (see Chapter 1) has to deal with in getting the family out of denial and into a useful supporting role for the child and the prosecution of the offender.

The Violent and Sex Offenders Register (VISOR)
Paedophiles are devious and persistent offenders. They are difficult to keep track of and are very good at blending into the background. Those with previous convictions are more straightforward to handle as a check against the Police National Computer (PNC), especially if supported by fingerprints, will identify them. The creation of the Violent and Sex Offenders Register was a logical step from the Criminal Records Bureau (CRB) check that is the first step in vetting applicants for jobs and positions working with children and vulnerable adults. The register is in fact a subset of the PNC. Under the Act offenders can be ordered by the court to register their addresses and any change of name with the police – failure to do so is an offence for which they can be imprisoned for up to five years.

The difficult people to manage are those suspected of predatory sexual behaviour but against whom there is not enough evidence to convict or against whom the school or institution concerned will not (for a variety of reasons) support a prosecution. Information against these people is currently held in a variety of systems and lists:

- police local intelligence systems (see Chapter 9)
- List 99, run by the Department for Children, Schools and Families
- The POCA – the Protection of Children List – and the SOVA – the Safeguarding of Vulnerable Adults List both of which are run by the Department of Health.

The problem with the current arrangements, as the Soham murders tragically proved, is that it is full of holes created by different standards regarding:

- the proof needed to be included on the list or system
- the time an individual should be kept on the list or system
- the degree of diligence in maintaining the list, updating it both with the entries and the particulars of those already on it.

These arrangements have been reviewed by Sir Michael Birchard and his recommendations have been implemented in the main by the Safeguarding of Vulnerable Groups Act 2006. In essence this will mean that all of the existing registers and lists will be amalgamated into one List of Barred Persons. The new list will be managed by the Independent Barring Board which will report to the Secretary of State for Children, Schools and Families. The implementation of this programme is now underway and is planned to be completed by 2010, by which time it hopes to integrate with the Impact system (local police intelligence). This will mean that police forces can check on an individual on all of the local intelligence systems in England and Wales. We have yet to see how successful this will be but the track record in amalgamating systems where the information comes from different organizations is not good and the Impact programme is already behind schedule.

Megan's Law
This is a law which was passed in New Jersey initially and now applies to most of the USA and has federal government backing. It created a responsibility for the local law enforcement bodies to inform local communities that a sex offender lives in the neighbourhood. In common with most other senior police officers and criminal justice professionals I do not advocate it be introduced in the UK as it does not improve the safety of children for the following reasons:

- determined offenders will not register so the only people the police and the community will know about will be those least likely to re-offend
- even if they register, persistent offenders will ensure that they stalk in areas where they are not known; there is no provision to inform the community under this approach and in any case it would be practically impossible
- it would diminish rather than improve the ability of the police and probation seervice to monitor those individuals who present the highest risk to children.

In my view the only safe way to deal with repeat paedophile offenders is to give them a life sentence so that they are only out of prison and in the community on licence and can be sent back to prison for any breach of that licence.

A final reason for opposing any such law is a combination of civil libertarianism and practicality. A provision like this provides ammunition and an agenda for any vigilantes in the community. There have already been at least two murders in the USA which can be attributed to this. Apart from the fact that not every sex offender deserves a potential death sentence one must also take into account the stupidity and gullibility of some members of the general public. It is highly possible that individuals will be mistakenly identified as paedophiles and will come under threat; anyone doubting the reality of this should remember the case a few years ago of the paediatrician whose home was attacked by a mob who believed he was a paedophile.

Robbery

This is a crime that seems to lend itself better to film than books. Most of the opportunities to obtain serious money from robbery have disappeared with the use of credit and debit cards, wages and pensions being paid directly into banks and the closure of post offices, especially at the edges of towns, which made the getaway so much easier. Those opportunities that exist are now much more difficult to attack and carry a higher element of risk because of:

- CCTV
- better security systems
- more professional security firms
- police helicopters (makes pursuit much easier and safer and avoids the problem of the cut-out – see below)
- automatic number plate recognition systems (see Chapter 9).

Most robberies involve at least one and sometimes two car changes, usually at a point where any pursuing police car is blocked off such as a pedestrian bridge or an underpass at a railway line. Any big robbery, such as the one at Brinks Mat, almost always requires both inside information and inside participation in order to get around the security systems. Detection of these robberies usually comes about through identifying the internal source and breaking them so that they put everyone in the frame in return for a lighter sentence (as happened with Brinks Mat) or through informants. Money-laundering countermeasures also help; again in the Brinks Mat case the Treasury noticed larger than usual amounts of cash moving through a Bristol bank and alerted the police.

A final point on robbery is the extensive misuse of the term. Robbery is stealing using force or the threat of force, so it is only possible to rob a person. Houses cannot be robbed, nor technically can a bank – the robbery is from the staff in the bank. If you break into the bank when there is no one there and steal the money, you have burgled the bank not robbed it (and you have certainly not burglarized unless you are in the USA).

Kidnapping

Kidnapping is a relatively rare crime in Britain mainly because the police have made it very difficult to get away with. Kidnapping for money (as opposed to partners abducting their own children from each other) is difficult to carry out for a number of reasons:

- the victim needs to be kept somewhere until the money is paid. This is not difficult for a short period

but becomes progressively more so as time goes on
- most people, even relatively wealthy ones, need time to get the amount of cash together that will make the risk worthwhile – which adds to the problem of keeping the victim
- two-way communication with the person providing the money (the target) is difficult without giving information to the police as well
- the pay-off is difficult to organize without the risk that the police will either make an arrest or pick up the collector and follow them either physically or technically (e.g. trackers in the bag)
- the money can be marked, making its future use difficult

We know that the crime is more prevalent in immigrant communities for a number of reasons:

- the target will have less faith in the police and will be less likely to involve them
- the likelihood that the victim will be murdered in the process is higher, so the threat is more real
- it may be possible to arrange the pay-off in another country, thus further subverting the usefulness of involving the police.

Since we only know of the cases where the police have been involved it is impossible to say how much of it goes on but this crime is an entrenched part of the culture in Turkey and Middle Eastern and Eastern European countries, which now have significant communities here, especially in London.

The major difficulty for the police is to have the target contact them in the first place. They then must maintain contact without alerting the kidnappers that they are involved. This means that all the initial contact with the target must be made covertly. It would be irresponsible for me to describe how this would be done but the one thing that would never happen is for a marked police car or people who were too obviously police to be sent to the target's home. We are fortunate in this country in that the media have agreed to a blackout of all information concerning any ongoing kidnapping and a number have been successfully thwarted because of this.

Terrorism

It would be easy to devote a whole book to terrorism, and if you need detailed information I would advise you to read the work of people like Nigel West and Richard Clutterbuck. Like most police officers who were never in Special Branch I have had little contact with the two security services, the Secret Intelligence Service (MI6) which deals with any external threat to the UK's interests, and the Security Service (MI5), responsible for counterintelligence and counterterrorism in the UK. Until relatively recently there was a clear division between the police and the security services. The latter developed intelligence here and abroad and the police were involved only if the intelligence exposed a spy or a subversive threat and prosecution was needed. Where the intelligence failed and there was a successful terrorist attack, the police would investigate it just like any other crime.

The picture began to change in the 1970s when the IRA and the Provisional IRA launched attacks on the mainland. This led some forces to develop an anti-terrorist capability, the Met having the most advanced because of the nature of the threat to the capital and the fact that it had the resources to do it. The peace process in Northern Ireland led to a decline in investment in the function to the extent that in 1996 the Security Service even made a bid for work by becoming involved in developing intelligence on serious and organized crime. The attack on the Twin Towers in 2001 changed all that. After the attack the security services in Europe and the USA realized the inadequacy of their knowledge of the Islamic terrorist threat and everyone moved their game up several gears, MI5 no longer showing any interest in organized crime.

The bombing of the Madrid railway and then the London Underground in 2005 brought the threat home to Europe and to the UK in particular. Any English force with either a sizeable Muslim community or a potential target will now have a significantly enhanced anti-terrorist capability, and be able to support the Security Service's drive to recruit informants and agents in these communities. The change is epitomized by the way that the Met has restructured its Special Branch, protection and anti-terrorist departments to create one Counter-terrorist Command (SO15), bringing together all the departments involved in security and counter-terrorism. Before this the Security Services would have opposed any possible amalgamation of Special Branch with the ordinary police tooth and nail in case it opened up their secret world to outsiders.

That said the two roles are still kept separate as far as possible, with the Security Services always owning the intelligence function and the police always being responsible for the investigation of offences and providing evidence for the prosecution. The difficulties that the separation can cause are:

- the Security Services always want the big picture and are more willing than the police to allow crime to be committed if this helps (their track record in Northern Ireland is a good indicator of how far they will go in this, even tolerating murder)

• the 'need to know' culture can leave the police investigator short of relevant intelligence at a critical point in the investigation.

The major gain is that the intelligence database is always one step removed from the police and so is less likely to be compromised by the disclosure needs of the prosecution (see Chapter 1).

CHAPTER 6

Organized Crime and International Policing

Organized Crime

Following the end of the Cold War, organized crime was described as the greatest threat to Western democracies. The Taliban and Al Qaeda's involvement in drug cultivation and trafficking compounds that threat.

There does not appear to be a universally agreed definition of 'organized crime' and it is more difficult to describe it in a UK context as we do not have the equivalent of the Italian or Russian Mafia, the Colombian or Mexican Cartels, the Japanese Yakuza, or the Chinese Triads nor the highly dangerous and violent motorcycle gangs of Scandinavia and North America. In London and one or two other cities we have, however, been exposed to the actions of the Triads and Jamaican Posses or Yardies and to the crime that shows you can always fool some of the people some of the time, the Nigerian-based 419 (the number of the relevant Nigerian statute) scam.

In Britain the tradition seems to be much less structured, with individuals or small groups being project-based, coming together for a specific operation or series of operations and then going their separate ways until the next project is proposed. The growing threat is from family clans of Kurds, Turks, Kashmiris and Pakistanis who use business and family links between the UK and their homelands as a cover for drugs and human trafficking, and the Russian and East European Mafias, but they have not yet reached the scale of any of the organizations described above.

The main areas for organized crime in the UK are:

- drug trafficking
- people trafficking for employment or sex
- smuggling (in the UK, apart from drugs it is mainly cigarettes, alcohol and counterfeit goods)
- fraud
- trade in stolen art
- paedophilia, especially pornographic exchange
- loan sharking
- car and plant theft (a modern tractor can cost more than a top-of-the-range Mercedes)
- counterfeiting – banknotes and goods.

The groups range from small city-based gangs to globalized transnational criminal organizations. It is difficult to take in the scale of activity. The UN estimated in 2000 that the gross returns from organized crime globally was between 1 and 1.5 billion US dollars. The profits of the Colombian cartels would comfortably sustain that country's national debt. From this it can be seen that these large organizations have the resources with which to take on the forces of law and order in technical, managerial and force-of-arms terms and that they have easily enough resources with which to bribe and corrupt at any level.

Most of these crimes are 'victimless'. The difficulty that

this creates is that there are no complainants to bring them to police attention. All the participants get some benefit from it. This can be true even of major frauds as they are usually directed against large financial institutions, which often prefer to suffer the loss than the adverse publicity. Where there are victims, such as in people trafficking and prostitution, they are rarely visible to ordinary people. Where they *are* aware of these crimes they are more often than not the purchaser of, say, prostitution. Of the crimes listed, only loan sharking impacts directly on individuals in the UK, but this mainly affects the poor and even then it provides them access to funds which are otherwise not available. Car and plant theft do have victims but they are usually covered by insurance, so we all pay.

Operational Features of Organized Crime
The nature and extent of organized crime can only be uncovered through the use of intensive investigative techniques, such as infiltration by undercover officers, the development of informants within the organization and sophisticated surveillance techniques using the whole spectrum of approaches, from officers on the ground through to the use of satellites – all supported by comprehensive and sophisticated intelligence collection and development techniques.

Even at the lowest level it is unlikely that these organizations will both be based and work in one police area. This is true even of the Metropolitan Police area, as the participants are likely to be 'housed' in the suburbs of Kent, Surrey and Essex but work both in the Metropolitan Police area and elsewhere in the country. This cross-border feature makes surveillance, the collection of intelligence and some operational deployment, such as with firearms or covert surveillance, at best cumbersome and often difficult.

114

These organizations are rich. This means that they can afford to infiltrate and subvert the government and law enforcement bodies, purchase equipment and people for their own protection against the state and other organized criminals, and develop sophisticated anti-surveillance techniques.

The people running these organizations tend to be clever. They are able to distance themselves from the actual criminal activities through layers of management and distribution organizations and the use of self-sufficient cells. They are highly 'surveillance-aware' in terms of both law enforcement agencies and other criminal organizations, and they have access to multiple identities, both personal and corporate.

They are willing to use high levels of force, including fatal force, if necessary. This makes the development of internal informants difficult and creates a very high risk threshold for undercover officers. Informants or witnesses must be supported by a sophisticated witness protection programme, both to ensure their safety and to encourage others to come forward. These programmes are expensive. They require sophisticated liaison with other organizations which have to generate and deal with the false identity, and a support programme which keeps the witness separate from family and other former connections. It also leaves the force open to a continuous stream of demands from the protected witness, which need to be resolved successfully if the programme is not to be undermined.

These criminals are highly mobile in terms of their ability both to move around nationally and internationally and to transfer their profits nationally and internationally. The creation of the European Union and its expansion has massively assisted in this in terms of personal mobility, and the removal of international barriers to capital movements has created a *laissez-faire* environment where the money launderer is spoilt for choice. It is relatively straightforward for those involved to remove themselves from jurisdictions in which they are wanted or suspected and to sustain themselves whilst abroad through the funds which they have already deposited there. They avoid those jurisdictions where controls are tight and they continually seek out the weakest links in terms of the risk of extradition and seizure of their money.

Those involved in medium- or high-level organizations are also engaged in legitimate business (although they may have been funded initially from crime). This makes it difficult to separate out legitimate from illegitimate profits and makes the issue of the seizure of assets a particularly difficult one, especially when the assets are in another jurisdiction.

As well as national and international crime there is also the problem of organized gangs working across the whole spectrum of activities described on a much more local and smaller scale – although still on a geographical basis wider than most forces and with the connections needed with these larger organizations to manage the local 'outlets'. All the difficulties that arise in terms of investigative powers, intelligence, surveillance, financial tracking and witness protection apply equally to this level of crime although limited to the narrower geography of the British Isles, with their different jurisdictions.

There are forty-three police forces in England and Wales, eight in Scotland and the Police Service of Northern Ireland (PSNI). Their operational response to organized crime will fall in the following areas.

Mobility
Even in a country as small as Britain operational mobility can pose serious problems. Scotland and Northern Ireland have different legal systems and devolved governments. This means that police officers do not have full police

powers outside their national jurisdiction and always require the co-operation and support of the local police in order to carry out any action. HM Revenue and Customs do not suffer from this restriction. The situation in the UK crystallizes the difficulty that will be met when trying to move the UK and other nations to a more transnational basis of policing (see below). England and Scotland have been united under one crown since 1704, and one parliament since 1807, but police officers only have full powers within their respective jurisdictions and, even here, when they are acting out of their force area will normally only act having informed the local forces of their intentions. Local chief constables still have an effective power of veto over other forces, although not the Serious Organized Crime Agency (SOCA), in terms of firearms operations or operations in those communities where sensitivities are high.

Surveillance
This is a very expensive police activity. In order to track a 'surveillance aware' suspect for sixteen hours a team of between twelve and sixteen is needed, depending on the likely movements of the suspect. Technical equipment and advance intelligence of likely movements can reduce this, but generally only at the margin. Most forces in England and Wales range from 1,600 to 2,500 officers. In Scotland, outside Strathclyde, they are significantly smaller. Other than the PSNI and the Met most forces have a very limited surveillance capability, usually limited to two or three teams. These generally have to cover the whole gamut of surveillance activity from serious criminals suspected of property crime such as robbery and burglary, through drugs, and increasingly in some forces, significant anti-terrorism work. Most officers are given basic surveillance training but the standard is variable.

Intelligence

Every force has a central intelligence bureau, but the bulk of the intelligence activity is carried out by basic command units and is focused at a very local level. Forces do not have open access to the SOCA systems but can only gain this through its operatives. This is not a criticism, as this is a necessary security and filtration gateway.

Financial Tracking and Seizure

This reflects the picture for intelligence and surveillance with each force trying to sustain small teams of variable ability through the ups and downs of budget changes and difficulty in recruiting to a very narrowly based task.

Liaison and Information Exchange

The UK is fairly unique in not having a national police force. Each force is independent and only the Met and Kent (due to the Channel Tunnel) have a real international capability. Indeed the absence of a national force leads foreigners to treat the Met as if it were one. This makes liaison difficult both ways and means that investigators are forced to work through SOCA, unless they have fortuitously managed to set up a bilateral arrangement with a foreign force. When this factor is combined with the sensitivities of all governments and judiciaries to foreign forces carrying out any tasks within their jurisdiction (see below), it puts the UK service at a particular disadvantage when dealing with matters which have an international dimension.

The National Crime Squad and the National Crime Intelligence Service

Until 1995 the UK had no national capability in terms of intelligence, surveillance or investigation. The highest level of capability was delivered by the Regional Crime Squads

(RCS) which had grown out of the task forces developed by groups of forces in the 1960s to deal with cross-border crime (depicted on TV at the time by Stratford Johns' Charlie Barlow). The work that the RCS encompassed became national rather than regional crime, and by the late 1980s it could be fairly said that the bulk of their work was either at a national or international level. By the early 1990s it was generally accepted that there was a need for a national body to deal with organized crime.

Internal police politics slowed the decision-making down and led to the illogical and dysfunctional decision to set up both the National Crime Squad (NCS) and the National Crime Intelligence Service (NCIS) as two separate entities. Both of these bodies continued to be staffed by recruiting police officers on secondment from forces.

The Serious Organized Crime Agency

The continuing growth of organized crime, particularly drug trafficking, and the increase in the terrorist threat and its involvement in the drugs trade led to another review and the decision was at last taken to set up a unitary body which could amalgamate the work of three agencies: police, HM Revenue and Customs and immigration, so that there was only one intelligence database and the problem could for the first time be given a strategic direction.

The agency was set up in 2006 and combines the powers of its three constituent parts, making it the most powerful policing agency in the UK. The Director can designate any of its operatives with the powers of a police officer, a customs officer or an immigration officer. It recruits from all three of these services, the Security Services and directly from the general public. Its operatives:

- can compel individuals to answer questions and

produce documents – not to comply is a criminal offence
- can strike deals with offenders to turn Queen's evidence – other agencies need the permission of the Crown Prosecution Service (CPS)
- have greater powers of confiscation than any other agency
- have greater powers to obtain court orders for the disclosure of financial affairs than any other agency.

It employs over 4,000 people and is divided into four directorates:

- Enforcement
- Intelligence
- Intervention and Asset Recovery
- Corporate (personnel, finance etc.)

SOCA is described as an 'executive non-departmental agency sponsored by, but operationally independent from, the Home Office'. The current Director-General is an ex-police officer but the Chair (supposedly non-executive) and three of the four heads of the directorates are all ex-Security Services. My guess is that this leaves the Director-General rather isolated and it is no coincidence that the police service already refers to SOCA as MI7.

Its main emphasis is on class A drugs and people trafficking, which together take up 70 per cent of its effort – 45 per cent on drugs, 25 per cent on people trafficking. This reflects the growing international nature of its work; it currently has 130 operatives working in forty countries. It also houses the Child Exploitation and Online Protection Centre and the National Central Bureau which links forces to Interpol, Europol and the Schengen arrangements (see below). The only service that it provides directly to forces is tactical and technical support in cases of kidnapping and extortion.

Crime-writing Possibilities
SOCA now houses two powerful cultures, which will inevitably clash. The police and customs culture which dominates the Enforcement Directorate will seek at some point to act in order to disrupt the criminal organization and take what it can; the intelligence culture which comes from the Security Services will always be striving for the complete picture, the gold at the end of the intelligence rainbow. The whole structure suggests that the intelligence culture probably dominates its current work and will certainly dominate its future. This is powerfully signalled by the way that success will be measured by the new agency. The NCS measured success by the number of organizations disrupted and the amount of drugs seized and assets confiscated. SOCA is to be measured on 'harm reduction' – whatever that may mean, and you can guarantee that it will always mean that it is succeeding.

There will also be tension between SOCA and individual forces. This may come in two guises. One is where the force is dealing with a criminal organization that is too big for its own resources and too small for SOCA – this will now apply to almost all criminal organizations that do not have an international element. The force will resent having to apply its scarce resources to a problem which is national or at least regional. The other situation, probably better in crime-writing terms, is where a force wishes to act and disrupt but SOCA would prefer to let the criminal activity run in order to be able to fill in the bigger picture.

There is also the possibilty of political interference. Chief constables are operationally independent and that independence has been clearly defined over time by the courts.

The Director-General of SOCA does not have that same operational independence. He or she is subject to political interference through the Board of the Agency (all appointed by the Home Secretary, who does not see the need for police representation) and the non-executive Chairman. Anyone who thinks that the Security Services are not subject to this form of interference has only to look at the 'dodgy dossier' for the Iraq war and its harassment of Labour politicians in the 1960s and 1970s for proof to the contrary.

International Policing

In the opening chapters of Dan Brown's *The Da Vinci Code* Captain Bazu Fache completely abandons a murder scene in which he had wiped out some important evidence and takes all his police officers in pursuit of a mobile phone, thus allowing Professor Langdon to escape. He then fails to catch a Smart car in which the professor is travelling in a chase through the Paris streets, traffic-free as it is early morning. You will see from this that he begins to look, in my eyes, much more like Inspector Clouseau than the 'tough, canny and persistent' character described in the Wikipedia entry. Then he invades England and allows Langdon to escape for the second time (by hiding in probably one of the easiest buildings to search, an aircraft hangar).

When reading the book this was the straw that broke this camel's back; the fictional world that Brown had created looked comical rather than mysterious. In real life police officers of any nationality enter into each other's patches with care and trepidation; for one to act in this way was laughable. If a police officer goes to make inquiries in another force he will normally get in touch with the local division, tell them the inquiries that he or she intends to make, check that it doesn't cut across anything that they are doing, find out if there is any local intelligence on the subject and possibly even invite them to be present. To carry out an investigation in another country takes weeks if not months of preparation and the involvement of the Foreign Office and requires the investigator to give the other country notice of whom they want to see and why. Although developments in Europe have eased the situation somewhat these basic requirements are still in place. The constraints, and the likeli-hood of future developments, are best understood by looking at the position in Scotland and England. The crowns united in 1704, the parliaments in 1807 and yet it is only in the last decade or so that they have grudgingly allowed each other's police forces limited powers in both countries.

One of the elements that distinguishes an independent state from any other form of governance is that government's exclusive right to use force or permit the use of force against any of its subjects or citizens. This means that governments are unwilling in the extreme to allow police officers from any other country to operate inside their borders. The power is jealously guarded so that, even when officers are allowed to enter another country in order to carry out inquiries, those inquiries are always either conducted by the police force of the host country or under its very direct supervision. This has long been appreciated by intelligent criminals who have exploited to the full the cumbersome mechanisms that police forces have to operate in order to make any progress.

Interpol
The first practical step to overcome this was the setting up of Interpol in 1923, initially by seventeen states not including the UK, but expanded in 1924 to include most of the countries of the then developed world. It was set up under the League of Nations and was based in Vienna. In 1938 when Austria

was invaded by Germany the headquarters was moved to Berlin and the organization quickly became defunct. It was reformed in 1946 under the aegis of the United Nations, initially being based in Paris and now in Lyons. It currently has a total of 186 member states, the highest number in any international organization. It is a peculiar organization in that it is not supported by treaty but is more like a private international association of chiefs of police, probably the reason why it has functioned in a very practical way.

From the very beginning Interpol's approach has been not 'What should be done', but rather, 'Given every country's different laws, culture, political maturity and approach to human rights what can be done?' All that can be done in this context is to exchange information. It would be impossible to get enough countries to agree that any international policing agency should have transnational policing powers of investigation or enforcement to make any arrangement viable.

Interpol has exploited its limited role very effectively. It has developed a database of passport information called Mind/Find. Through this any passport can be checked against its database at any border crossing in real time. It now has a very extensive database of more than 120,000 files concerning people, vehicles and stolen art and has its own secure communication system which allows open access to all the members through its Automatic Search Facility (ASF). This strength is also a significant weakness. A large number of the countries which are members have corrupt governments and police forces. Any police officer putting intelligence on the system knows that these forces and governments have access to it, so most of the information which is held is either low level or is targeted at individuals rather than criminal organizations. For example it would be idiotic to put sensitive drugs intelligence about the trafficking of cocaine from Colombia through Venezuela then East Africa when all of these countries have access to it.

Every member of Interpol has a National Central Bureau (NCB), which can be a large unit, as in all European countries, or just one nominated person. In the UK the NCB consists of a detective superintendent and fifty-nine staff, twenty-one of whom are police officers. All the country's inquiries are handled by the NCB, although the ASF can theoretically be extended out to police forces and even down to the individual if the country has a secure communications network (which the UK has). For practical reasons of security, audit and sheer manageability the UK, and most other countries, limit the access to the ASF to the NCB.

The bulk of Interpol's work is done through its system of notices. These are either generally circulated or specifically aimed at targeted countries. In 2007 6,000 were issued. They are colour coded:

- red – descriptions of persons wanted for arrest and extradition
- blue – descriptions of persons whom one or more countries seek to locate and trace
- green – descriptions of persons of interest to one or more countries
- yellow – descriptions of missing persons
- blue – unidentified bodies.

Within its limited terms of reference Interpol is a highly effective and very valuable organization, allowing police forces some operational capability in the international sphere.

Europol
Europol is still a bit of a character in search of an author. It was born out of the then EEC's TREVI arrangements of the

1970s which are now so arcane that there is no agreement on what the acronym means (although there is a majority view that it means *terrorisme, radicalisme, extremisme et violence internationale*). It was a logical product of the growth in trade and cross-border movements in the Community. When the EU was formed by the Maastricht Treaty, what later grew into Europol was established by the creation of the European Drugs Unit, based at The Hague.

Any proposals to develop an international European police force face the same sovereignty issues that limit Interpol. Some countries with a strong federal background such as Germany are more relaxed about such a proposal and Chancellor Helmut Kohl proposed that such a force be established in 1990. Most other countries are more reluctant to cede police powers in this way. Given Britain's reluctance to join even the Schengen arrangements, our resistance to any concept of a federal state of Europe and our history of relations between Scotland and England, it seems highly improbable that any force will be allowed to operate in the UK in the foreseeable future. This resistance has been compounded by the rapid expansion of the EU in the last decade to include a significant number of countries from Eastern Europe, some of whose police forces have a very poor reputation in terms of corruption and human rights.

Europol's current status is that of a European Interpol in that it is restricted to developing databases and exchanging information, although it is now expanding its work into training and support, particularly for the new member countries.

The Schengen Agreement

The Schengen Agreement was signed in 1985 by France, Germany, Belgium, Luxembourg and the Netherlands. It committed those countries to open borders, with the free movement of people and commerce without passports or customs barriers. It was not actually enacted until 1995, when it was also signed by Portugal, Spain, Italy and Greece. It now applies to all the EU mainland countries except Bulgaria and Romania and also includes the non-EU countries of Norway, Switzerland and Lichtenstein. The UK and Ireland are not signatories but already have their own Common Travel Area which allowed free movement without passports. Both limited their participation in the Schengen arrangements to improved political and judicial co-operation.

The open borders on the mainland created a need for greater police co-operation, providing for situations of 'hot pursuit' and surveillance operations where the subject crossed a border whilst being followed. Those provisions are:

- Police forces can continue 'hot pursuit' across the border provided that they are in uniform and are in a marked vehicle. They can carry their service weapons. They have limited powers of arrest and common sense dictates that the further the pursuit goes into the second country the more likely it is that that country will want to take over the operation completely
- They may continue a surveillance operation where the subject has crossed the border. If possible they should obtain permission first but in cases of urgency they can do so without permission provided that they tell the second country of the operation as soon as possible. The second country can either permit them to continue the operation or tell them to terminate it. If consent is not obtained within five hours the operation must be terminated. They may carry their service weapons during the operation.

Although these provisions look very limited they are significant in terms of improved police effectiveness and the political maturity of the signatory countries. Indeed the Schengen countries have achieved in twenty-five years what it took the UK 300. The signatory countries have also developed a criminal intelligence database to which the UK and Ireland have access.

Bilateral Contacts

Police culture is such that trust is usually based on personal contact or references from trusted sources. This applies to both police forces of the same country and international contacts. The more sensitive the intelligence, the more certain any police officer likes to be of its recipient. It also helps if the forces have similar cultures. This has meant that over the years policing in Europe has divided into two: the north – i.e. the UK, Ireland, Germany, the Netherlands and the Scandinavian trio of Sweden and Denmark and Norway; and the southern – Greece, Italy, Spain and Portugal, which have a reputation for more deep-set corruption. France seems somehow to bridge the gap between the two. To these two have now been added the Eastern European countries, which are still fledgling democracies and whose police forces have poor reputations. A British police officer would be unlikely to wish to work with or give intelligence to anyone in these countries whom he or she had not personally worked with or whose credentials he or she could not establish with another trusted officer.

In crime-writing terms a bilateral friendship is easily the best device to use in allowing an investigator to operate in a foreign country. It allows the protagonist to act under the aegis of the police force of that country, with all that that means in terms of powers and access to intelligence. The growth of transnational policing operations (especially in drugs, money-laundering and organized crime), international conferences and shared training have all made the development of such friendships more likely and thus more credible.

Inquiries Outside Europe

Forces do send officers abroad to carry out inquiries. It is a very expensive process and is only used for very serious crime such as murder or kidnapping, when the force believes that it is the only way of getting the information. In England it is done through the Foreign Office. If they accept that it can work they will approach the government of the country concerned to establish whether they are willing to receive police officers and assist them in carrying out their inquiries under what is called a *commission rogatoire*. The investigating team have formalized terms of reference from which they cannot diverge. During their inquiries they will always be accompanied by a senior member of the police force of the host country, who can direct that all inquiries be made through him or her. The formality, the language problems, the differences in culture and the need for the investigators to stay within the terms of reference mean that the overall effectiveness is crucially dependent on:

- the state of relations with the receiving country
- the effectiveness of its police force
- the culture of the country with reference to co-operation with the police
- the relationship between the investigator and the local police officer in charge.

We had a very good example of how this can and might not work in Bedfordshire, with the murder of a Kashmiri. He had been shot in his restaurant with a shotgun and the car the assailants had used was found burnt out some distance away. There were no forensics and we were sure that it was a 'domestic', i.e. that it was an inter-family issue. We sent officers to Pakistani Kashmir, to the village where the victim came from originally. What worked was that the investigator established a very good rapport with his Pakistani counterpart and we found out what had almost certainly happened. What didn't work was that the information was all hearsay and we doubted that a British court would have approved of the methods that the Pakistani police used to obtain it.

Extradition

Whether or not a person can be extradited from another country is crucially dependent on:

- the existence of a bilateral agreement between the two countries
- the crime being recognized in the extraditing country
- the crime being included in the agreement.

The process is now relatively straightforward within the European Union but can be very difficult elsewhere. For example the Russian constitution will not allow the extradition of a Russian citizen. As an ex-police officer I find it ironic that the USA, which consistently refused to extradite members of the IRA during its bombing campaigns of the 1970s and 1980s on the grounds that their crimes were political, will now, after 9/11, kidnap individuals for 'extraordinary rendition'. It makes one realize just how flexible even a written constitution can be when there is the political will.

CHAPTER 7

The Use of Force

In law the justification for the use of force is essentially very straightforward. Much of the confusion which exists has resulted from the need for the media to create headlines and punchy sound-bites. Under the common law and statute the police can use reasonable force to carry out an arrest, prevent crime, prevent an offender escaping and subdue riotous behaviour.

The use of force must be 'reasonable' in two ways:

- the circumstances must support the use of force, e.g. the suspect resisting arrest or refusing to desist from riotous behaviour
- the degree of force must be reasonable in all the circumstances.

Human rights legislation states that it must be proportionate and in the second context that is probably the better word: the officer's use of force must be proportionate to the threatened or actual use of force by the suspect. The measure of proportionality is shown in Figure 5. At the lower end of the continuum the officer may be able to control the situation merely by telling everyone to behave, if necessary backing it with the threat of arrest if they don't. At the top end of the spectrum will be the suicide bomber where the level of force used will almost certainly be fatal.

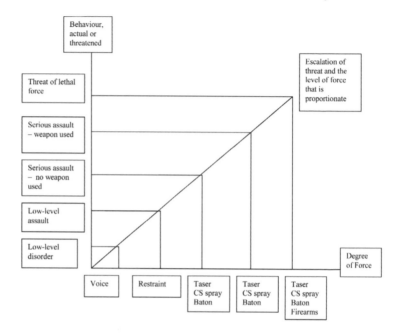

Figure 5: The Use of Force Continuum

You will see from this that tasers (when electrodes are fired at the offender and paralyse him or her briefly through delivering an electric shock) and CS spray are both seen as being a lower level of force than the use of a baton. This is because they both have no lasting effect whereas the use of a baton can cause serious injury and has been known to be fatal.

The police objective at every stage along the continuum is to remove the threat. At the lower end of the graph the threat is removed when people begin to behave themselves, but for the suicide bomber it is only removed when he or she is no longer able to detonate the bomb.

What Is Reasonable?

This brings us on to the issue of reasonableness. The test of 'reasonable in all the circumstances' comes in two parts:

- Was it reasonable for this officer in these circumstances to use force at all?
- Was the degree of force used reasonable, i.e. proportionate to the threat?

The first question is answered by looking at the officer's decisions subjectively, i.e. from his point of view, with the knowledge that he had at the time. The second question is answered objectively, i.e. would the reasonable person – in law 'the person on the Clapham omnibus' – think that the degree of force used was reasonable and proportionate?

The Officer's Viewpoint
In deciding whether it was reasonable for the officer to use force the question that must be answered is not 'Would the person in the street or would I think that it was reasonable?' It is, 'In these circumstances, with the background and knowledge that they had, was it reasonable for this officer to use force?' As far as stopping a would-be suicide-bomber is concerned the court would need to consider the following:

- how real was the threat? If there had been other recent instances that day or that week, for example, then the level of threat would be high
- what was the officer's belief that the person was a suicide bomber based on? If it was merely casual observation and no weapon was seen or threat made then it would probably not be justified. If it was the

result of a detailed briefing concerning a specific threat by a named or described suspect then it would probably be justified.

This is so even if the officer is mistaken as to the facts – e.g. if he or she believes that someone is armed but it turns out to be a replica or even an object that only looked to them like a gun. As long as the officer believed it was one the use of force is reasonable. The same applies to any belief that the person was fitted with a suicide bomb.

The Degree of Force
The second test of reasonableness is an objective one and is probably more straightforwardly dealt with by asking, 'In the light of what the officer believed the level or type of threat to be, could the police objective have been achieved by a lower level of force?' If the answer to that is yes then it is probable that the degree of force used was unreasonable; if no it is probable that it was reasonable. A good example is an armed police officer confronted by a man wielding a large knife thirty to forty feet away from the officer, who continues to attack despite being warned that armed force will be used. In these circumstances it would be possible for the officer to get close enough to ensure that he could shoot to wound in the upper leg before the knife became a real threat. If the same thing happened in a confined space where a shot was difficult and the probability of disabling the knifeman was low then a body shot could be justified, despite its probable fatal consequences. Similarly if the officer believed that he or she was faced by a man armed with a gun, the only reasonable option would be a body shot (the biggest target), as it would be essential to remove the threat, i.e. the man's ability to fire the gun at them or a member of the public.

Suicide bombers present a new and unique threat. They are resigned to dying and their sole intention is to take as many people as possible with them. When the threat is considered in this light it can be seen that the only viable option to the officer is a head shot, probably firing several times. There are two reasons for this. First, since most suicide bombers carry the bomb as a form of waistcoat a body shot may detonate the bomb. Secondly, it is essential that the bomber's ability to use the trigger be negated as quickly as possible, so the shot selected must be the one most likely to cause instant death or at least paralysis. Only a head shot can achieve this. Even if this is successful the officer is still seriously under threat as the bomber may be using a 'dead man's handle' type of switch – one where the bomb is activated if the bomber loses their grip on the trigger.

You will see from this that the police do not have a policy of 'shoot to kill'. The policy is and always has been one of removing the threat using only that level of force which is proportionate to it. The use of the modern extended metal baton is likely to break a bone and will definitely cause a traumatic injury to a muscle but no one says that the police policy in dealing with rioters or hooligans is to break bones (much though a significant number of the public wish it were).

The Use of Force by Civilians

The legal use of force by civilians arises under three circumstances: carrying out an arrest, preventing somebody from committing a crime, and self-defence. Section 3(1) of the Criminal Law Act 1967 provides that 'A person may use such force as is reasonable in the circumstances in the prevention of crime, or in effecting or assisting in the lawful arrest of offenders or suspected offenders or of persons unlawfully at large.'

The fundamental difference between civilian and police powers is that for civilians a crime must have been committed or be in progress whereas a police officer need only suspect that a crime has been committed and that the person arrested might have committed it. Just like the police a civilian can use reasonable force to effect an arrest and the test of its reasonableness is the same as that of the police. Police do not encourage civilians to get involved in arrests, however, for two reasons. First, they have no training in the techniques required to subdue using minimum force and secondly, and probably more importantly, in getting involved they may endanger their own safety. In addition in low-level issues such as minor assaults where the parties are known to one another it can be the devil's own job to sort out who did what to whom first.

The most common use of force by civilians is in self-defence. For a long time the law required that the person threatened should show a willingness to retreat, but this is no longer the case. Civilians are entitled to use reasonable force to protect themselves or others for whom they are responsible, and their property. But it must be reasonable. The test is the same as for the police:

- What was the level of threat?
- Was it reasonable for this person in these circumstances to feel threatened?
- Was the force used proportionate to the threat?

The CPS has a very good record for allowing considerable latitude where the threat is real and the circumstances exceptional – e.g. confronting a burglar in one's own house. There have been many cases where the degree of force used by the householder was excessive but allowance was made for the effect that an intrusion of this nature would have on the victim. That said there must be a threat. For example in the case of Tony Martin it could not be said that a young man running away represented a threat to someone holding a shotgun and there certainly could be no justification for shooting at his retreating back. If it is done deliberately to harm him and he subsequently dies the crime is one of murder; if the shooter is reckless of whether or not the person is hit it is manslaughter. In Mr Martin's case the finding of murder was reduced to manslaughter owing to his defence of diminished responsibility.

The Wikipedia entry 'Self-Defence in English Law' is very good on self-defence.

CHAPTER 8

Police Miscellany

As a reader I find the way that writers get very simple, easy-to-research issues about police wrong very frustrating. Taken far enough they can burst the 'bubble' of the world that they have otherwise successfully created. The particular issues for me are:

- police discipline, especially the issue of suspension
- senior officers
- police culture
- informants
- representative organizations.

Discipline and Suspension

There are two routes by which a police officer can be the subject of discipline – internal, where a supervisor has found him or her behaving incorrectly and invokes formal disciplinary procedures, and externally where a complaint has been made by a member of the public. If there is evidence of wrongdoing both end up with a formal hearing before an assistant chief constable and two superintendents.

Until 1998 police officers were governed by regulations

which had changed very little since Victorian times. This listed specific offences, such as drinking on duty, and was based on the military model of discipline rather than the civilian one, despite the fact that police officers are civilians who wear uniforms just to get the job done. Any allegation needed to be proved to the criminal standard of proof, i.e. beyond a reasonable doubt, rather than the usual one for employment law of being proved in the 'balance of probabilities'. The regulations were reviewed and the list of offences was thankfully abandoned. A code of conduct was introduced which requires that police officers should be honest, impartial, polite, obey orders, only use reasonable force, etc., and any breach of the code can be subject to formal discipline.

The standard of proof was also changed to be the same as in employment law – the balance of probabilities – a change that I had campaigned for as chief officer as I believed that the issue was one of employment and not criminal culpability. In most complaints against police it is only the complainant's word against that of the officer. The criminal standard of proof meant that many instances of unacceptable behaviour went unpunished and the officer stayed in the job. The Police Federation argued that the police had to deal with criminals, often in difficult situations, who would make malicious allegations against them, so the burden of proof should be higher. This argument garnered considerable public support at the time, but it is specious for two reasons. First, the case will be judged by police officers, who will be well aware of the danger and sympathetic to the officer. Second, the fact that someone has a criminal record will seriously undermine their credibility as a witness, so weighty corroboration will be needed. In addition the more serious the outcome the greater the weight of evidence needed – you need a lot more for murder than for a speeding ticket.

Suspension

This is a very formal procedure and is still used fairly rarely, usually only if the presence of the officer on duty may be detrimental to or hinder the investigation, or where it is in the public interest. Because of the seriousness of the consequences everything that can be done to avoid it will be done, including restricting the officer to a non-operational role. No officer is ever suspended by the Chief Constable in person. The Chief Constable will be the final arbiter in the disciplinary process, and so can play no part at all in the investigation of any offence or complaint. It is always done by an officer from the Complaints and Discipline Office, which is usually called by some euphemism these days, including Professional Standards Office (Thames Valley), Internal Affairs (Greater Manchester, watching too much TV) and best of all the Directorate of Professional Standards Customer Service Team (the Met, getting in every buzzword possible). The formality of the occasion is such that this officer will read from a prepared script, giving the accused officer the details of the allegation and the reasons for the suspension. He or she will get a written copy, usually referred to as a Reg. 9 notice.

In crime writing, having protagonists restricted to a non-operational role is in many ways preferable to suspension as they will have access to all the force's resources and can go to and from police stations and police units. A suspended officer cannot do this; indeed until fairly recently they were banned from all police premises, even social and sports clubs.

Most sergeants and inspectors will only use formal discipline as a last resort. The nature of police work provides a whole range of 'punishment' postings for officers who cross them in some way – boring jobs that might entail standing around in the rain, keeping guard on premises or guarding prisoners in hospitals. In contrast, training and other exciting postings are held out as a reward for good work. In all my time as operational police officer I never felt the need to initiate formal disciplinary proceedings nor did any of my colleagues.

Complaints

Most police officers get into trouble through a complaint made by a member of the public. The police are duty-bound to record and investigate every complaint, no matter how trivial. Minor matters such as those concerning an officer's manner and attitude can be informally resolved if both the complainant and the officer agree. Where appropriate officers can be invited to apologize but they cannot be made to do so, nor can the force apologize on their behalf if they do not agree. In most non-urban forces this type of complaint makes up the vast bulk. In busier urban forces the position is usually quite different; the majority of complaints are allegations of criminal conduct, such as planting evidence, perjury, assault and malicious prosecution.

The complaints process is now overseen by the Independent Police Complaints Commission (IPCC), which was set up in 2004. It is the latest in a line of bodies which have gradually increased the degree to which complaints against police are independently investigated and adjudicated. The major changes brought about by the IPCC are:

- the oversight of the whole process – previously the Police Complaints Authority only reviewed more serious cases
- the introduction of non-police investigators – until 2004

all complaints were investigated by police officers with the Police Complaints Authority supervising the more serious ones.

The IPCC classify and manage complaints in three categories:

- a supervised investigation – the force will be responsible for the investigation and will report on its progress and completion to an IPCC supervisor
- a managed investigation – the force will provide the investigators and the IPCC supervisor will decide how the investigation will be carried out
- an independent investigation – the whole investigation will be carried out by independent IPCC investigators.

The category to which a case will be allotted will depend on its seriousness and the public interest.

Senior Officers

The following is the rank structure up to Chief Superintendent, which applies to all forces.

Constable
Sergeant
Inspector
Chief Inspector
Superintendent
Chief Superintendent

Above the rank of Chief Superintendent, the structure in London differs from that outside the Met area. Outside

London, the structure is as follows:

   Assistant Chief Constable
   Deputy Chief Constable
   Chief Constable

In London (both Metropolitan and City forces) it is as follows:

   Commander
   Deputy Assistant Commissioner
   Assistant Commissioner
   Deputy Commissioner
   Commissioner

Note that the ranks of Chief Commissioner and Assistant Chief Commissioner, much loved by writers and journalists (particularly the BBC for some reason), don't exist. 'Detective' is a designation of the type of job done and only denotes membership of the CID; it is not a rank. So an inspector and a detective inspector have the same rank, and who will be in charge will depend on the circumstances – if investigating a crime, the detective, if dealing with a public order incident, the uniformed inspector. (The situation can be different in US forces, as they often have grades of patrolman and detective, and the move to detective is clearly a promotion.)

In order to understand the rank structure it is necessary to give a brief description of how most forces are structured. They are divided into basic command units (BCUs). These are geographical divisions, usually co-terminous with local authorities, which are big enough to provide 95–98 per cent of policing needs and small enough to be managed by one person, usually a chief superintendent.

Their size varies from around 250 officers to as many as 1,000, although the latter are usually subdivided in some way – which seems to defeat the original object of a unitary command. In the police, as in most organizations, there appears to be a cycle of change taking you remorselessly back to where you came from, and I note that some forces are already beginning to call BCUs divisions – the term that was scrapped fifteen years ago in favour of BCU.

Force headquarters are divided into departments which are usually described as operational and administrative support. The former will encompass functions such as traffic, firearms teams and headquarters CID; each function is headed by a chief superintendent and groups of functions will come under the control of an assistant chief constable. Administration will include finance, personnel and training, which will be headed by a mixture of civilian and police managers. Every force has a website and a writer can easily find out this basic information on one visit; even an imaginary force will have a real-life equivalent which can be used.

The last truly operational rank in uniform, on duty 24/7, face to face with the public, is inspector. Those above inspector have operational responsibilities but spend most of their time on management tasks. Each division and department will have a call-out rota for these ranks in order to cover out-of-hours calls for more serious incidents or where a firearms operation is to be mounted. This means that the constable's senior officer is usually the shift, relief or office inspector; the inspector's is usually the chief superintendent. BCU officers will rarely meet anyone above the rank of chief superintendent.

Until the 1980s most forces ran their CIDs as headquarters departments so that those based at a station still reported to and were managed by the detective chief superintendent at headquarters. That changed, and the divisional (now BCU) commanders were given control of their own CIDs. That is still the case except where a murder or other major incident is being investigated, where the investigation team will almost inevitably be made up of officers from all over the force and control of the investigation will come under the direct control of the senior HQ detective.

The profile of the chief officer team – the assistant chief constable (ACC), the deputy chief constable (DCC) and the chief constable (CC) – varies from force to force. They are commonly referred to as the ACPO team from their membership of the Association of Chief Police Officers. In some forces the culture is that the ACPO team often visit BCUs and carry our regular patrols with officers. This was my preferred approach and it is surprising how relaxed and informative officers can be if you share their task with them for a few hours. Some forces are the opposite. In one force in which I served we only saw one of the ACPO team if there was trouble or we were about to be inspected by Her Majesty's Inspector of Constabulary (HMI). One chief I know of had two nicknames: the Eternal Flame, as he never went out, and the Chinese Chief Constable, Mr Who.

From my perspective the rank which always seemed to have the biggest impact on the public was chief inspector – superintendent sounded more like someone in charge of a public lavatory and many members of the public had real difficulties with the 'constable' element of assistant, deputy and chief constable.

A final point from the perspective of a writer. All chief constables were at one point in their careers constables, then sergeants, then inspectors and so on. They have probably done most of the jobs that their officers are doing and will have pulled, or seen pulled, every scam at every rank. In real life they are very knowledgeable about what is going on in their forces and usually very empathetic to the problems their officers face. Most importantly, they can read between the lines of reports and make a good guess about what really happened, no matter what the report says.

Culture

Police culture has changed significantly since the 1970s when *Life on Mars* DCI Gene Hunt, although a bit of a caricature, could be said to exemplify a lot of the culture at that time – boozy, chauvinist, macho and very 'can do'. Much has changed since that time, but much has stayed the same. Women still only make up 20 per cent of the police officers and are still not fairly represented in specialities and senior ranks. Despite the targets set by the Home Secretary following the Macpherson Report, which said that forces should represent their communities, none of the big four (the Met, West Midlands, Greater Manchester and West Yorkshire) has come anywhere near the target. The Met has been the most successful with 8 per cent, against a target that is closer to 25 per cent.

The majority of the service is still recruited from the white, male working-class, and the culture will reflect that, in the same way that society itself does in terms of language and attitude towards issues such as equality of opportunity. The language out of the public view can be ripe with expletives, especially when things are tense, and the humour, as in all three emergency services, is black – as pitch sometimes.

Each of the functions tends to reflect the type of person attracted to it so that:

- Patrol reflects the fact that it includes everyone from those who have just joined to the thirty-year veteran.

The older constables, especially if they are any good at the job, will have a tremendous influence on how a shift or relief operates. Of course the shift is the home of the 'canteen cowboy', who has been everywhere, seen everything, done everything, but no one can remember when he last made a decent crime arrest.

- CID is probably the most varied now, but until the early 1990s it was almost exclusively white male. It tends to reflect the cynical edge of policing, and detectives still tend to have the poorest marriage record and the biggest drink problems (when this gets too bad they are sent back to uniform).
- Traffic is mainly male and is staffed by men who like driving big fast cars and motorcycles – a bit like *Top Gear* without Jeremy Clarkson's subtlety and political correctness.
- Firearms units tend to have a larger number than usual of ex-services personnel, and the culture is probably closer to that of the army than the police in many ways.

Informants

These are an essential element of policing and yet appear to be little used in fiction. People usually become informants for one of three reasons:

- revenge – the disgruntled ex-wives or girlfriends are often a very good source of regular useful information
- money – this is not usually the major reason as the money paid out by police is usually quite modest, but it is often associated with the following factor
- control – this informant tries to manipulate the police

to take out a rival, leaving the field clear for them. This scenario is often accompanied by an unhealthy or corrupt relationship between the informant and the handler.

An old detective once told me that with informants either your foot is on their neck or their foot is on yours. They're dangerous people and should only be handled or developed by experienced officers. Every force, in theory at least, has all its informants registered and the relationship between them and their handlers is monitored. No officer is allowed exclusive handling rights on any informant, but must share them with at least one other officer, usually a sergeant or inspector. That said, the competition in CID for the best arrest record and detectives' drive to be in control of their job and their fate will inevitably mean that some of them will still do their best to keep their informants exclusive for as long as possible.

Representative Organizations

There are four elements of the police service which are represented in some way: three police and one civilian. Union membership tends to be low, especially in the smaller forces, and civilians are represented, if at all, by Unison. In my experience the civilians working for the police are highly committed and rarely threaten industrial action and relationships between police management and the union are usually good.

The police themselves have three levels of representation.

Chief officers (assistant, deputy and chief constable) are represented by two organizations – ACPO and the Chief

Police Officers Staff Association (CPOSA). ACPO does all the policy development work and will represent the senior officers' view to the government and the public. It works on the basis of consensus, and although it has done a lot to professionalize its working – it now has a president who serves for four years rather than one – it is still a bit slow on its feet compared to the Police Federation (see below), which often purports to represent the 'police' view. CPOSA negotiates chief officers' terms and conditions of service.

Superintendents are represented, not surprisingly, by the Superintendents' Association. Except for the period just after the Labour government was elected in 1997 they have had little influence on policy development.

Police officers are not allowed by law to strike. This law was passed following police strikes in London and Liverpool in 1919 – the situation in Liverpool became so anarchic that the government actually sent gunboats. As a result the government removed police officers' right to strike and be members of trade unions. Instead it created by statute the Police Federation to represent officers from constable to chief inspector. This body is highly professional at representing its members, both at a local level in terms of disciplinary proceedings and at national level in terms of negotiating pay and conditions. It has a deserved reputation for being able to run rings around Home Office civil servants and uses its considerable bank balance and position to influence politicians and the community at every level.

CHAPTER 9

Technology

This chapter heading seems slightly pretentious, as my limited knowledge will only allow a brief, non-technical description of the most common technology used by the police today.

The Police National Computer – PNC

This began life in the early 1970s as a computerized record of stolen vehicles but it now incorporates a number of useful databases, and is accessible at any time.

Criminal Names
This has details of all convicted, cautioned or recently arrested persons (nominals). It lists recent convictions, gives a description of the subject, including identifiers such as scars and tattoos, and shows previous addresses and any previous co-defendants. The file can be searched using the Querying Using Extended Search Technique (QUEST – I don't make these names up, I only report them) using elements of the record such as height, age, etc.

A nominal can also be marked as 'wanted' if they are sought in connection with the crime, or they can be marked as 'of interest'. Both will show the officer who wants the subject arrested or is interested in him or her and the officer's station and force. It has links to the Automatic Fingerprint Recognition (AFR) system and the DNA database and is now accessible to the Schengen database (see Chapter 6).

Vehicles

This file has details of registered owners, the vehicle's tax status, and its chassis and engine numbers. It is updated every day from the Driver and Vehicle Licensing Agency (DVLA). It has a police element which shows if the car is stolen or is of police interest and what the officer interested wants done – whether they just want to know when and where it has been seen, or whether they want it stopped to identify who the occupants are. A search can be carried out on a partial description using the Vehicle Online Description Search (VODS) – a boon in major inquiries, where partial registration numbers and descriptions are common. It is linked with the Motor Insurers' Bureau database which gives the details of the policyholder, and with the DVLA MOT database.

Drivers

This file gives details of all licence holders, their endorsements and whether or not they are disqualified. It is also updated daily from the DVLA database.

Property

This file holds a limited amount of information on property, usually that which can be identified through a serial or registration number, such as engine plant, trailers or firearms.

Local Intelligence Systems

Too many people both in and outside the service use the term 'intelligence' without giving any thought to what it means or how it can be differentiated from other similar words such as information, facts, knowledge etc. I have developed a model which I have found useful:

- data – single elements of fact/rumour concerning criminals or criminal behaviour
- information – enough data to make an analysis possible, producing some hypothesis concerning the criminal or their behaviour
- intelligence – a hypothesis which is firm enough to act on

For example, X owns a car, registration number ABC 123 (data). He has been seen driving to the south of London twice a week and has sometimes been seen in London contacting a known drugs dealer. Rumour has it that he is developing his own dealership locally (information). The hypothesis is that he goes to London to stock up twice a week, so the next time police can wait at his addresses and stop and search the car on his return from London (intelligence).

All forces have had to develop their own stand-alone systems to record and analyse this data, since the government had been unwilling to fund the development of a central facility. Computer support is needed for three reasons: first, it takes an ocean of data to produce a trickle of intelligence; secondly, a computer system can be made available at all times to officers in the field to both record and retrieve information in a way that a card- or paper-based system cannot; thirdly, one force's system can be made available to another through a secure landline. The National Police Improvement Agency is currently developing a programme called Impact which aims to link all the existing systems. It was due to be completed by 2010 but is already behind schedule. From the difficulties that arose in the investigation into the Yorkshire Ripper case and the failings of intelligence in the bombings of the London Underground one would think that the weaknesses in this approach would be only too obvious to the Home Office, but they have alway been short-sighted when it comes to leadership in this area and it is probable that the situation will be allowed to drift on until the next disaster.

Custody Systems
The whole custody and prosecution process is now computerized. This has led to less paperwork for officers and easier management of the information contained in it. A major operational gain has been that these systems incorporate a digital camera, so that when prisoners are photographed a digital image is captured. This means that the photograph database can be searched automatically on description, making it much easier to limit the number of photographs shown to witnesses and making the probability of a successful identification more likely.

Automatic Number Plate Recognition Systems
These were used for the first time on any scale by the City of London Police to help them manage the 'ring of steel' erected around the city during the Provisional IRA's sustained attacks in 1992 and 1993. The system allows the car registration number to be checked in real time against the PNC so that its status can be verified. Successors of the system are now used by most forces. The tremendous improvement in digital image quality and the reduction in

the cost and size of computers means that they can be used proactively to track offenders and gather vehicle-related intelligence. This is important as most major acquisitive crime, such as drugs trafficking and burglary, requires the use of vehicles, so an ability to carry out remote surveillance without having to use people is invaluable. It has also meant that traffic cameras can process prosecutions almost completely automatically; when it was first introduced the courts complained about the additional unmanageable workload and the number of prosecutions had to be artificially limited.

CCTV

Britain is reputedly the most watched country in the world in terms of CCTV coverage. All town centres, shopping malls, major railway stations and bus terminals are routinely covered by them. The information they provided in the failed attack on the London Underground on 21 July 2005 vividly shows their value to the police. The first systems were analogue and the images they produced were poor. This problem was compounded by bad management. Tapes were used too often so that already poor images became useless, and sometimes they were reused immediately rather than being kept for a set period, in case they contained information whose importance was only realized later. Most systems are now digital, which has significantly improved the quality of the image and made it cheap and easy to store the recordings for a reasonable period of time (a month).

The major current drawback is the number of officer hours that viewing them takes when trying to find information about an incident. For example, if two men are seen walking away from the location of a car bomb wearing hats and hoods so that the camera cannot see their faces, it is necessary to keep expanding the sweep of the systems viewed in the hope that they will have been picked up by a camera when they are far enough away from the scene to relax their vigilance, perhaps allowing a view of their faces or some other identifying factor such as getting into a car or using a cash machine.

Facial Recognition Systems

These are less common and are still in the process of development. The theory is that if you already have a digital image of the target all you need to do is attach the facial recognition software to a digital camera or digital recording and it will make the match, or at least reduce the number of images that need to be physically searched to a realistic number. If the software could do it accurately then the match could be made in real time – an enormous operational gain. The police now have a vast bank of digital images of people arrested and if they are sufficiently interested in someone who is not on that database it is a simple task to go and get one through surveillance.

So what's the problem? It's all a matter of geometry. Nearly all cameras are mounted quite high so as to maximize their range and minimize their intrusiveness. This means that key distances and angles in the image captured, such as between the eyes, between the nose and the upper lip, or the length of the nose and face, will all be different from those in an image where the shot has been taken at the same level as the subject. It is possible to compensate for this to some extent but there is no standard height or angle of image capture so that the current systems are limited to those where it is possible to mount the camera to capture the subject 'face-on'. A further complicating factor is that photographic features can be affected by changes in light and the background against which the photograph is taken.

Mobile Phones

This is not really technology used by the forces so much as technology used by the public which provides enormous operational and investigative assistance to the police. Mobile phones work through a series of cells and a record is kept of which cell or cells any particular phone is using during a call. This allows the phone to be tracked, in real time if there is an operational need, and the times and recipient of the calls are also recorded. A significant number of people have been convicted for causing death by dangerous driving because it has been possible to show that they were using their mobile phone at the time of the collision.

Mobiles give two other benefits. First, they are really just radios, so it is possible to pick them up on a scanner and monitor what is being said without a warrant, as is needed to monitor a landline. Secondly, although professional and even low-level criminals are aware of the danger of using mobiles which they minimize by using re-carded stolen phones and pay-as-you-go contracts for short periods before either re-carding them again or dumping them, they still tend to keep all their numbers stored on the current card or keep them on a personal phone – the convenience outweighs the danger. This is a goldmine of information if the police can get their hands on it.

Surveillance

Police make extensive use of technology for tracking and surveillance – the GPS systems used in cars show how small these devices can be and how they can enable the police to track the target vehicle or person accurately and easily. Similarly micro CCTV cameras make bugging relatively straightforward and formidably easy to install and conceal. If you intend to use these in any detail in your plot I would advise you to consult sites on the Internet.

Helicopters

The major gain from the use of helicopters in terms of technology is their thermal imaging capability. This has revolutionized the service's ability to work after dark and has resulted in the capture of innumerable criminals, especially burglars and car thieves, who would almost certainly have otherwise made good their escape.

Satellites

What about the satellite surveillance that is commonly seen in fiction such as the TV series *24* and films like *Enemy of the State*? Anyone who thinks that this capability is available to the police only has to consider the case of the Washington (or Beltway) sniper. For a period of three weeks the sniper shot at random targets, usually while they were carrying out some mundane task like filling their cars with petrol or mowing the lawn, killing sixteen people and injuring two. If there is any city in the world which is likely to have a guardian satellite it is Washington yet the police worked initially on the wrong vehicle, a white van, and called in an aerial reconnaissance aircraft. In the end the snipers were caught because a member of the public became suspicious on finding them sleeping in a blue Chevrolet saloon similar to the one later circulated by police.

CHAPTER 10

Relationships with Other Agencies

The Crown Prosecution Service (CPS)

Legal systems in the developed world have two main bases, the English Common Law and the Napoleonic Code. In essence while the Code is followed by most of continental Europe and in French dependencies and former French colonies, the English Common Law is the basis for legal systems in the Commonwealth and in the USA. The Napoleonic Code gave the power to direct inquiries and initiate prosecutions to investigating magistrates and in the USA the office of District Attorney was developed, taking responsibility for prosecuting offences and directing police inquiries. Rather uniquely, this is usually an elected rather than appointed post, which brings with it all the potential for corruption that goes with the political process. In England on the other hand anyone could lay information before the magistrates and begin a prosecution. As a result, until 1987 the police were responsible not only for all the aspects of investigating offences but also for prosecuting them, employing lawyers where necessary, just like any other litigant. In Scotland the Procurator Fiscal is responsible for prosecutions and can direct police inquiries. This may be due to the way that the Scottish law developed before the eighteenth century, when there was a strong bond between Scotland and France.

The CPS has come on the scene quite late compared to other prosecuting authorities and, on the face of it, lacks the glamour and powers of its Scottish, continental and American counterparts. Relationships between the CPS and the police were initially strained, partly because there was resentment in the police that their authority had been diminished in that they no longer took the decision to prosecute, and partly because the CPS was seriously under-resourced and had great difficulty in handling its caseload efficiently.

In recent years the situation has changed considerably. The CPS is now well established and handles its workload efficiently. Although it does not have the power to direct police inquiries it is now involved at an early stage in the investigation of serious or complex offences and it would be a rather naive and arrogant investigating officer who ignored any advice that the CPS gave. If the investigator does not do as the prosecutor asks it is likely that the prosecutor will subsequently decide not to proceed, or not to proceed with the charge that the officer would prefer. The key to successful working relies on personalities and the fact that the prosecutor is now a part of the investigation process creates a situation which can be exploited by writers in terms of tension and conflict.

The Fire Service

Relations between a police force and its local fire brigade at a very senior level are usually very good. At street level there always seems to be some tension for reasons that have never been clear to me but I have witnessed it in both the English and the Royal Hong Kong Police. In both it seems to have arisen out of two issues: unionization and precedence. At the beginning of the twentieth century both services developed trade unions but following the police strikes in 1918 and 1919 the police were forbidden by law from joining trade unions and the Police Federation was created. This has inevitably led to situations where the police have either substituted for firefighters directly or assisted the military to do so when firefighters have taken industrial action.

The more likely reason for the tension is the issue of precedence. Until relatively recently the fire service resented the fact that the police were recognized as being in overall control of emergencies and there was a concerted move by the brigades to change the situation, so that they were in charge. It is now resolved that the fire service is responsible for the immediate scene of any emergency – putting out the fire and facilitating the rescue of people trapped – but that the police remain in overall command. This is logical for three reasons. The first is that the police have the numbers and the infrastructure to deal with large emergencies which require the setting up of command areas and rendezvous points and facilitating the fire and ambulance services into and away from the scene. Secondly, if there are any deaths the police will be responsible for investigating them, either reporting their results to the coroner or conducting prosecutions. Thirdly, any prosecution will almost certainly be based on a forensic examination of the scene. While the fire service has some limited capability here they do not have the depth of experience and knowledge necessary to do this effectively and, crucially, they will not be responsible for all the other enquiries, such as insurance fraud, nor for any subsequent prosecution.

The NHS

Most police officers would say that the relationship with hospitals and GP surgeries is great when the police are doing something for them but they are not very good at returning the favour when they want them to do something. Most casualty departments are grateful when police officers include them in their patrols in the late evening, especially at weekends, as it reminds the drunks who make their life difficult that there is a police presence and that there may be a penalty for abusing or assaulting staff. Similarly the police are used routinely to trace and contact relatives, to escort transplant material, etc.

The difficulty arises when the police look for some sort of quid pro quo, usually looking for information on someone who has been treated for an injury. NHS staff then retreat, in most cases perfectly appropriately, behind patient confidentiality. But the fact that it may be justified doesn't make it any easier to accept when you know that they have information that would greatly assist your inquiries. Another point of conflict is where a prisoner needs medical treatment. The doctors and nurses are very uneasy at treating a prisoner in the presence of a police officer, and there is usually much discussion before it is finally agreed that the officer needs to be there for everybody's safety, not least that of the general public.

The Judiciary

Police are now very much at arm's length with the judiciary, both crown court judges and magistrates. This has always been the case with judges as it is rare for police to meet them anywhere other than a courtroom and, unlike some fictional judges, in real life they are only too willing to restrict their activity to the courtroom. The relationship with magistrates used to be different when police presented their own cases in court, as active officers would appear frequently and would over time develop a relationship with the bench, especially if it was a stipendiary magistrate. Now that all the cases are presented by the CPS and as much as possible is done to encourage a guilty plea, often on a lesser charge, in order to save everyone's time, police officers have very little contact with the judiciary.

Local Government

Most of the issues concerned with the prevention of crime in a strategic rather than tactical sense are under the control of local government – education, town planning, social services, youth service – so it is not too surprising to find that there is extensive contact between police and local government agencies at every level. At senior level they work together in the Community Safety Partnerships which organize a whole gamut of activities, amongst which probably the most important is the implementation of the government's drugs strategy.

Where police have established either neighbourhood policing teams or problem-oriented policing (POP), this relationship will extend all the way down to street level, tackling problem hotspots in a multifaceted way. Police have been involved in schools for a very long time. This can extend to officers being members of governing bodies, or even being posted permanently to some of the very big inner-city comprehensives. The other major involvement is around domestic violence in its many forms: child abuse and attacks on wives or partners. After a shaky start in which the social workers and medics worried about the police being too prosecution-minded, officers are now an integral part of the case conferencing process and most forces now have units dedicated to family protection.

Central Government

There is very little contact between police forces and central government, even at chief constable level. My experience is that the senior mandarins treat police officers with a mixture of wariness and condescension, the latter increasing as one moves from the Home Office to the Foreign Office, and reaching its peak with the Treasury (which I believe is the way they treat each other).

POSTSCRIPT

When I meet other developing writers at conferences and courses and they find out that I have been a police officer, they inevitably ask me which crime writers I like and what makes their writing work for me. I will preface my remarks by saying that if I had 10 per cent of the talent of these writers I would probably be published by now. They're successful because they are good writers, their characters live on the page, they engross me as a reader in their world, and only every now and again do they get it so wrong that I have a quick intake of breath before going on.

Of the British writers my favourite is probably Ian Rankin (and not just because he is a fellow Scot), although his protagonist, John Rebus, is the antithesis of a good police officer in that he keeps all his information to himself, not even sharing it with his closest partner Siobhan, and he has a drink problem that would worry any senior officer who was relying on him to deliver the goods. Rankin, however, is careful not to get involved in the detail of policing – I don't think I have ever read of Rebus making a formal arrest – but his description of the police culture, particularly their attitudes and language, is the closest reflection of real life I have found in any writer. His last three books have been his weakest, in my opinion, as the need to stay outside the constraints of police procedures has required fairly extreme artificiality in the plotting. My favourite books are *Dead Souls* for its darkness and *A Question of Blood* for the intricacies of the plot and sub-plots.

I also like Val McDermid's Dr Tony Hill. Her characterization is always strong and the people live in my mind long after I have finished the story. Her plotting and pace are excellent and she makes good use of the device of having a police officer running in parallel with her main protagonist (Jonathan Kellerman also does this in his Alec Delaware series). This allows him to have access to all the support systems available to the police, such as forensics and the PNC, while allowing her main character the freedom to work outside formal procedures.

No list would be complete without P.D. James. Dalgliesh, initially a detective chief inspector and latterly a commander, is like no police officer I've ever met. A poet and aesthete, he is at the opposite end of any spectrum you could consider from DCI Gene Hunt from *Life on Mars*. She succeeds for me in the way that she makes characters interact, in the intricacies of her plot and in her ability to involve me and sustain an interest in Dalgliesh's melancholic musings. Like Rankin I think she has let the character run for too long and she has needed to create increasingly artificial environments in order to allow her to involve Dalgliesh, a Met officer, in events outside London. I think that the high point of her writing was *A Taste for Death*.

The last British author I will mention is Peter Robinson. I believe that he comes closest to getting the procedures right and he makes good use of them to move and channel the plot. When I was invited to run a workshop I wrote to several authors asking them how they view procedure. P.D. James, Minette Walters and Peter Robinson were kind enough to reply. He said that the way he came at procedure was to ask not what should be done but rather, given that this is what I want to do, how can I do it? I believe that this is the right approach, although in order to satisfy yourself about what can be done it is necessary to know what should be done so that you will know just how far from reality you are travelling and how to structure the story so as to fit.

I am probably more comfortable reading police procedural crime which is based abroad, like the books of James Lee Burke and Michael Dibdin, as I know very little about police procedures in either the USA or Italy and thus the story never jars if the author gets it wrong. I doubt that a police officer like Dave Robicheaux exists anywhere in America. He is violent and a recovering alcoholic, spends significant parts of books being suspended or under threat of arrest and has as a best friend a homicidal maniac. But the plots are superb, the language poetic and the dialogue sharp and darkly humorous.

Michael Dibdin's Aurelio Zen is at the other end of the spectrum. Like Rebus he is inclined to melancholy and has difficulty in establishing worthwhile relationships with women but the underlying black humour, the dialogue and the sheer lunacy of trying to work in a society where it is impossible to know who is really in charge is engrossing.

Finally there is Henning Mankell and his detective inspector Kurt Wallander. I doubt that anyone with such a consistently depressive approach to dead bodies could survive for very long in police work (although maybe it is different in Sweden where it is dark for so much of the year and alcohol is too expensive to be enjoyable) but you can't help feeling sympathetic to all his woes and Wallander's plots keep you involved until the end (except *The Dogs of Riga* in which his raid of the Latvian police archives is frankly ludicrous).

Glossary

ACC	Assistant Chief Constable
ACPO	Association of Chief Police Officers
AFR	Automatic Fingerprint Recognition system
ANPRS	Automatic Number Plate Recognition System
ASF	Automatic Search Facility
BCU	Basic Command Unit
CC	Chief Constable
CID	Criminal Investigation Department
CPS	Crown Prosecution Service
CPOSA	Chief Police Officers Staff Association
CRB	Criminal Records Bureau (was Criminal Record Office (CRO) run by the Met until it was made a stand-alone agency)
CSO	Community Support Officer
DC	Detective Constable
DCC	Deputy Chief Constable
DCI	Detective Chief Inspector
DI	Detective Inspector
DNA	Deoxyribonucleic acid
DS	Detective Sergeant (sometimes also confusingly Detective Superintendent although in the police this is usually abbreviated to D/Supt.)

FSS	Forensic Science Service
GHB	Gamma-Hydroxybutyric acid (date rape drug)
HMIC	Her Majesty's Inspector Constabulary
HOLMES	Home Office Large Major Enquiry System
ID	Identity (parade or card)
Impact	Project to interlink local intelligence systems
IPCC	Independent Police Complaints Commission
IRA	Irish Republican Army
LCN	Low Copy Number testing of DNA
LIO	Local Intelligence Officer (formerly called the Collator)
Met, the	The Metropolitan Police
NCB	National Central Bureau
NCIS	National Crime Intelligence Service
NCS	National Crime Squad
PACE	Police and Criminal Evidence Act 1984
PCR	Polymerase Chain Reaction (in DNA testing)
PIP	Professional Investigation Process
PNC	Police National Computer
POP	Problem-oriented policing
PSNI	Police Service of Northern Ireland (formerly the Royal Ulster Constabulary – RUC)
QUEST	Querying Using Extended Search Technique
SCRO	Scottish Criminal Records Office
SIO	Senior Investigating Officer

SOCA	Serious Organized Crime Agency
SOCO	Scene of Crime Officer
STR	Short Tandem Repeats (in DNA testing)
'Sus'	Suspected person under the Vagrancy Act 1824
VISOR	Violent and Sex Offenders Register
VODS	Vehicle Online Description Search

Useful Internet Sites

Every police force now has a website and can be easily accessed through any search engine. I have also found the following sites useful.

Crime Library
www.crimelibrary.com
A US site with lots of information which either inspires or depresses.

Home Office
www.homeoffice.gov.uk
A good source of basic information on police, drugs etc.

Interpol
www.interpol.int

Murder in the UK
www.murderuk.com
A good source of basic information.

Police Oracle
www.policeoracle.com
A site which looks as if it is aimed at police groupies and wannabees or those deluded officers who describe themselves as 'street warriors' but it has a good file on police

slang (be careful how you use it as if it is out of date your writing is only pitiful and not atmospheric) and police humour.

Serious Organized Crime Agency
www.soca.gov.uk

Thin Blue Line
www.policensw.com
This is the web page of the New South Wales police in Australia and it has excellent files on fingerprints and forensics.

UK Acts of Parliament
www.opsi.gov.uk
This has all the acts from 1990 on and is being added to. It is useful for confirming what you know but not good for searching for information.

Wikipedia
www.wikipedia.com
I have found this facility to be excellent and the reference sites enable you to check and confirm or question the information given.

INDEX